Control or Freedom?

Control or Freedom?

Volume 1

Dr. Simon Atkins, PhD, DSc

Sale of this book without a front cover is unauthorized. If this book is coverless, it may have been reported to the publisher as "unsold and destroyed" and neither the author nor the publisher may have received payment for it.

Lhatong Publishing Mass-Market Edition, March 2014

© 2014 by Dr. Simon R. R. Atkins, PhD, DSc
All rights reserved.
Published in the USA by Lhatong Publishing, LLC.

Skyaia® is a registered trademark of Dr. Simon R. R. Atkins.

Cover art / design by Joe Kawano and Author Sensei.
Full permission to use cartoons by Larry Lambert.

Cataloging-in-Publication Data is on file at the Library of Congress.

ISBN-13: 978-0-9960218-0-7
www.skyaia.com
Printed in the United States of America
10 9 8 7 6 5 4 3 2 1

The author of this book does not dispense medical advice or prescribe the use of any technique as a form of treatment for physical, emotional, or medical problems without the advice of your physician, either directly or indirectly. The intent of the author is only to offer information of a general nature to help you in your quest for emotional and spiritual well-being. In the event you use any of the information in this book for yourself, which is your constitutional right, the author and the publisher assume no responsibility for your actions.

This book is sold subject to the condition that it shall not, by way of trade or otherwise, be lent, re-sold, hired out, or otherwise circulated without the publisher's prior consent in any form or binding or cover other than that in which it is published and without a similar condition including this condition being imposed on the subsequent purchaser. No part of this publication including any illustration may be reproduced, stored in a retrieval system, or transmitted, in any form or by any means – electronic, mechanical, photocopying, recording, or otherwise – without prior written permission.

For information: Lhatong Publishing, LLC; 1302 24th Street West, #355, Billings, Montana 59102 USA.

Namaste to all.

It is an honor

for the Universe

to have guided you

to these pages.

Table Of Contents

Dedication i
Meaning of Lhatong ii
Important Definition & Warning iii
Literary Notice: A Few Words Of The Truth viii
The Author, In The Raw x
Skyaia® Blog xiv
Special Note On Book Design xv
Acknowledgments xvi

Part 1 ♦ Transform Self

Preface 4

Chapter 1 7
Skyaia® Theory

Chapter 2 21
Connected Beyond Our Dreams

Chapter 3 37
No Ordinary Shift

Chapter 4 51
Cosmic Change & Health Impacts

Chapter 5 65
Our Destiny Depends Upon Your Mind

Chapter 6 83
Realizing Our Birth-Given Right To Freedom

Chapter 7 99
Plug In To Divine, Your Connection To Energetic Source

Part 2 ♦ Connect To Skyaia®

Chapter 8 119
Your Path Is The Key

Chapter 9 135
The Climate Change Scam

Chapter 10 151
Global Weather Volatility And Planetary Change Hotspots

Chapter 11 171
Advanced Climate Control: Electromagnetic Technology, Weather Warfare & Radiation

Chapter 12 213
Lowering Your Immunity & Controlling Our Minds Through Weaponry We Cannot See

Chapter 13 231
Avoid The Scare Tactics, Embrace The Sun

Epilogue 241
When Other Objects Appear In The Sky

Special Note 251
Skyaia®: Blinded or Awake? Volume 2 - To Be Published Soon

Recommended Books / Papers, A Short List 255

Control or Freedom?

Dedication

To two beautiful children, Skye (8 years young) and Gaia (6 years young) – who chose me in this lifetime to be their father, and who together respectively represent the energies above us – from the sky to the cosmos to other universes, allowing us to dream and spread our energetic wings – and – the energies within and below us to allow us to ground and center ourselves with our home, Mother Earth.

To you, my awakening reader – with this book in your hands, I extend my gratitude for your energetic sustenance, and humbly invite each one of you to analyze, research, learn, empower, share and expand your quest, journey, path and new discoveries all in positive light and for the greater good of humankind and its united consciousness.

Meaning of 'Lhatong'

A Tibetan word meaning 'superior vision' or 'panoramic visualization' (as in multi-dimensionally).

It refers to the experience of form as emergent from emptiness, or to meditation methods that aim to find that experience.

IMPORTANT DEFINITION & WARNING

Once you see the connections between the Establishment, our climate, your health including the threat of radiation and fear of cancer, other cosmic life, and so much more, you will never see the world the same again.

The energetic vibration that is opposite of the Establishment is the pulsation of Skyaia®. While Skyaia® represents gratitude for life and the energetic connection between each other as brothers and sisters, the Establishment's aims are surrounded by eugenic goals and philosophies of the Occult. While Skyaia® teaches that the path of the mind and connection to the cosmos is the true way to realize Abundance, the Establishment is developing powerful technologies to control our mind so that we become energetically-shackled slaves unable to progress to our true spiritual heights that were intended by the Universe.

This is about our destiny. This is about our choice. And you definitely can help the human race make the right decisions.

'Establishment' is used a lot in this book because it is the negative way the world is 'run' or 'governed' (through increasingly dictatorial rule), and is central to the theme of the future of Global Emancipation Citizens United, in winning the War on the Mind – the last frontier that the Establishment wishes to control – a conflict that begun in 1993 in almost an alternate world bridging ours, but because much of the Mainstream Media is State-controlled, it has yet to be "understood" by the majority of We the People.

There is a war going on inside the USA this time. Not just in the USA the Corporation, but in the USA the Republic. You might not see it at first, but since you have been guided to these pages, you are learning of it or are an "expert" in discussing many facets and phases of the predator and prey. This confrontation is between the Government as is shown / as we know it, and rogue factions of the government (which is anti-Constitution, anti-freedom, eugenics-based). Parts of this war are spilling-out into the American economy, through or by major corporations, and into society at-large, with the goal to control We the People at the new level of evolutionary consciousness transitioning our planet at this time.

This book, *Volume 1: Control or Freedom?*, will describe at times the Establishment, and what We the People (as per the Declaration of Independence, and other proclamations of freedom in other countries) are up against in the struggle against tyranny.

This process of tyranny and new "energetic" enslavement is happening not only in the USA, but in other parts of the world too. Fortunately, however, this Establishment Agenda is not happening in all countries. There are "havens of peace" and an increasing number are seeking these all the time. But timing is of the essence, as it has always been.

THE ESTABLISHMENT

Refers to either one or all of the following (and I request that you do research on any number of them to see their 'record'):

- the oligarchic elite,
- Opus Dei and the Knights of Malta,
- the Elite Forces,
- the "invisible government" or the "shadow government"

consisting of Committee of 300 (aka the Olympians), and other international councils that work for or beside it like the Club of Rome, the Trilateral Commission, the Royal Institute for International Affairs (RIIA), Socialist International, the Council on Foreign Relations (CFR), and over a hundred others scattered around the world,

- the Farnese family and descendants
- the Military Industrial Complex,
- the Federal Reserve Bank (not federal and not a bank)
- Big Pharma (and the criminally-run Military-Medical-Industrial Complex, and the international medical-pharmaceutical cartel)
- the Bilderberger Group; Rothschild / Rockefeller families,
- the Vatican (Shadow Government),
- DARPA and other sub-military deep-research wings
- Planted insiders in government entities like NASA that don't report to anyone within that organization and are in-charge of mainly controlling information to the outside (for example, air-brushing space images before release to the public so all orbs and other entities are taken-out)
- factions and individuals advocating, financially supporting and marketing eugenics programs in the past and present (like Bill Gates, Milton Katz, Willy Brandt, Joseph Rettinger, and many others),
- the NSA
- the FDA, FEMA, the IRS, the United Nations, DHS

(Department of Homeland Security – who has loyalty to the United Nations), and other conspiratorial umbrella organizations that are used as 'fronts' by higher-up's,

- Tavistock institutions like the Brookings Institution, Flow Laboratories, Rand Research and Development Corporation, National Training Laboratories, and many others,
- some heads of the corporatocracy,
- fascist leaders,
- the Illuminati,
- royalty (the power behind the throne),
- patrimonialists,
- the United Nations (and their Agenda 21)
- secret societies like Bolshevism-Rosicrucianism, the Order of St. John of Jerusalem, the German Marshall Fund, the Cini Foundation, the Round Table, the Milner Group, the Fabianists, the Venetian Black Nobility, and the Mont Pelerin Society,
- authoritarian and totalitarian regimes,
- breakaway factions of a government (e.g., a potential coup d'état even within the U.S. Government),
- Black Op or Psy-Op events,
- False Flag events,
- clandestine sectors of government-run agencies, and
- the One World Government / New World Order.
- … and there is so much to tell …

Remember, this book is all about your awakening, our Awakening together, and everything about the lies vs. Truth, the Dark vs. the Light, and the de-evolution vs. the individual progress that we, the People, can attain.

But there is a key: we each have to know what is truly happening by joining the 'pieces' together like a huge jigsaw puzzle. And we have to not only know what we want, but we have to declare it, not only physically and verbally, but also energetically, vibrationally and telepathically – through our mind connection to collective united consciousness.

Welcome to Skyaia®.

LITERARY NOTICE: A FEW WORDS OF THE TRUTH

Lhatong Publishing, LLC would much rather any profits from the sale of this book to go to good causes such as helping the disadvantaged, into research and toward the expenses of both attaining and sharing higher knowledge with enlightened souls of this planet, rather than have to hire a bunch of attorneys to protect Dr. Simon Atkins from frivolous and potentially lengthy and aggravated lawsuits from the Establishment or other negative beings that may see any of his stated written words as potentially contentious. The author realizes it is necessary to be prudent, and that since this is 2014, not a hopefully more advanced civilization of peace in 2042, these statements are included to pertain to any word, group of words, or expression of thought contained within this book from front cover to back page:

- Lhatong Publishing uses, at times, psychologically graphic and potentially disturbing ways to describe current situations, events, places, and institutions. Lhatong Publishing states and demonstrates scientific, technological and medical evidence and academic substantiation.

- This is not a conspiracy theory.

- The writing style and even sense of humor, at times, may be either extremely funny or downright revolting, depending on a person's education, background, beliefs, and ability to think multi-dimensionally. I, the author do not apologize for any bluntness; I call a fork a fork.

- Any conclusions drawn by the reader may be completely opposite beyond those stated. Lhatong Publishing does not intentionally mean to offend in any way. Any insinuations, ideas, evaluations, allusions, intimation or other expressed interpretations of anything written in this book are of Lhatong Publishing, and are granted full protection by the First Amendment (Amendment I) to the United States Constitution (and is otherwise grandfathered in if in months or years to come either the Constitution of Bill of Rights no longer exist). For those who might have been told by liberal professors or other talking heads including those in the media that don't appreciate their freedoms that the Bill of Rights is no longer necessary or important, the First Amendment prohibits impeding the freedom of speech and/or infringing on the freedom of the press, amongst other important things.

- Lhatong Publishing and Dr. Simon Atkins individually and collaboratively do not promote or intend to imply or represent that anything said in this book can prevent, cure, treat or mitigate any disease or class of disease. We must all realize that it is the body and connection to Mind that heals oneself. Dr. Simon Atkins has personally benefited from the evidence presented. Any statements herewithin have not been evaluated by the [corrupt] Food and Drug Administration (FDA) [because this unit of the Establishment is not knowledgeable or capable to look beyond certain boundaries of oppression of health and decreased liberty]. Any product or method described within does not come with any promise to diagnose, treat, cure, or prevent any disease [but you would be wise to empower yourself by researching into the possibilities stated because they show extreme shining strength in working effectively].

THE AUTHOR, IN THE RAW

Dr. Simon Atkins is a climate risk economist, a planetary threat forecaster, solar expert, and energy medicine doctor. His new field is biometeoelectromagnetics™. Simon is also an informant for the People, a spiritual pacifist and modern-day monk. Call him a "compassionate fighter" for freedom, with a goal to move the planet forward.

Born in Rugby, U.K., at 9:34 a.m. on May 13, 1969, Simon was raised in England until the age of 11. Then, his father made a pivotal decision to move the family to New York in 1980. After Simon got his B.Sc. in Atmospheric Sciences from Ivy-League Cornell University, he accepted a position at Weathernews Japan and swiftly moved to right outside Tokyo in 1991. Then in 1993 he went to Finland to attain an International MBA. It was at that point that the seed of Advanced Forecasting Corporation began. After teaching business at Hawaii Pacific University and receiving his USA citizenship in the mid-90s, he returned to NYC after a short failed marriage.

In late 1998, he met by happenstance a wonderful person at a bus stop at JFK Airport outside NYC. That person (& her mother) helped to change Simon's life, allowing him to re-decipher the meaning of life and everything he had learned. The answers to his quest for truth about the origins of human life, climate and cosmic energy, healing, disease, natural health, and more – all related back to energetic expression – became more recognizable.

Right before 9/11, Simon had what he calls a significant 'clairvoyant moment', and was guided to move to Montana. In late 2002, he met Yoshie. After six weeks of dating, he proposed, and three weeks later they got married in the mountains of Wyoming. In 2004, not wanting to move, Simon started his Ph.D., thanks to distance education. When Skye, their son, was born in the spring of 2005, Skye soon developed a ringworm / pus-like growth spreading over his face. Simon's naturopathic studies really took off, and in lambasting a dermatologist's advice to put their infant on steroid medication, he and Yoshie instead began a journey with their naturopathic physician in Billings where the doctor found a natural treatment and Skye quickly healed. In the middle of Simon's doctoral studies, their daughter, Gaia, graced the world on Xmas Eve in 2007.

In another moment of out-of-body lucidity late in 2009, Simon realized that dis-ease can be transformed and healed by a shift in mental, emotional, physical, spiritual and energetic vibrations. In this Near Death Experience (NDE), he connected a few more of the dots of the life journey, and not only successfully conquered a long course of fibromyalgia through natural & energetic means, through the help of a group of ND's, but become conscious of the reality of two amazing things: 1) many energy flows like climate patterns and even our mental states can be shifted by both natural and technological modification in electromagnetics; and 2) cosmic or alien life is abundant on Planet Earth and has always been a part of the ecosystem here in various forms.

In 2010, Dr. Simon set course to complete a second doctorate – this time a D.Sc. in Alternative Medicine. He chose an institution of learning out of India – the birthplace of energy medicine – and thanks to the vision of the school, Simon combined climatic energetics and its effects on health into a new field of the future that he has named biometeoelectromagnetics™.

Nowadays, Simon is sought all over the world for his sharing exciting solutions in climate, business, health and Individual

Freedom. He is known for his passionate, lovingly blunt and dynamic appearances on a host of issues from minimizing risk in climate change and planetary perils, optimizing natural health through manifestation of positive energy circles, and becoming unwired through "Connective Logic" – a method of ungluing yourself from the brain-twisting Establishment, unhooking yourself from the "Big Brother monitor", questioning everything, becoming self-sufficient, and joining the dots to attain your true freedom to discover real joy and abundance.

A Special Message To Those Destined To See These Pages

No matter what others may say to the contrary, Simon urges all individuals to follow their dreams, goals and most of all, their intuition, no matter how unique that path may be.

Simon has come to the realization that we are each a light be-ing wrapped in a shell. He says that the most fundamental and significant connection in this lifetime and any past existence or successive journey beyond Now is with a higher, more evolved (but not superior) energetic form. You may call this God (Elohim), Source, Universe, One, Christ, Mohammad, Tao, Buddha, Archangel Michael, or any other religious or spiritual name. Simon says that on your quest in your lifetime it is important to make sure that that Voice (aka your Higher Self) and its influence does not cause you to cower from your true purpose, nor live in fear, and never be manipulated negatively or otherwise contact you in any form other than through an energetic vibration of heart and love.

The ideas enclosed within have the potential to really change your life for the positive. You, the reader, may do what you intuitively feel is important.

In the days we live in this lifetime, the Establishment may instigate and try to take away additional abundance from any of us because the Establishment fears two things: first, that the planet can move forward in a positive way, and second, that we, as individuals, may attain more freedom than at present through an awakening of collective mind command potential. When you block negative energies, like those coming from the FDA and other ego-tripping individuals and organizations, you can intent freedom and positive flow in your life such that abundance and love will sustain you and allow you to be victorious in all challenges in life.

From one energetically connected be-ing, from me to you as another, I radiantly bless your God-Self.

Please connect through:
Twitter: @DrSimonAtkins
Blog: www.Skyaia.com

P.S. This book's written style is only that of the author's; editing has been cut to a minimal because it was agreed that the author wanted this to be an authentic piece of his passion to express the research, insights and ideas / solutions from his unique perspective. To that regard – thank you, especially to grammar kings and queens [said in humor], for your tolerance if a single sentence continues on for six lines, or if a concept is not initially explained correctly.

SKYAIA® BLOG

www.Skyaia.com

… never fear-mongering, never sensationalistic … an alternative collection of intelligence on the subjects of climate, health, planetary risks, technology, investments, socio-economic threats, and related issues, ideas, and insights … to help gain you an 'edge' in the onslaught of news, and always substantiated with news links from around the world …

Please sign-up for this free blog column at www.Skyaia.com.

I look forward to keeping in touch with you about the acceleration of our Awakening, many important / related things in the contents of this book, and future volumes of Skyaia®.

◆

Thank you.

Special Note On Book Design

Book Cover Art

I marvel at the impressive abilities and insights of a group called Author Sensei – Rivka, Joe and Karah. Joe "gave birth" very naturally to this wonderful book cover and Karah and Joe made sure that the interior formatting was professional. Rivka and Karah, with their "feminine power", continue to make sure that all ideas and direction, including the marketing through Twitter and other social media, is intuitively balanced to get us all connected. The team also worked every step from start to finish to make the Skyaia® Book Video Trailer. I highly recommend their wonderful talent!

For information about book design or marketing help, please visit their site at www.AuthorSensei.com.

Cartoons

I give my most enthusiastic thanks to Larry Lambert, the cartoonist. Larry designed some new cartoons especially for the themes on this book. You will quickly realize that the sarcasm in each cartoon is brilliant.

Through the cartoons, I trust that the overriding theme for you, the reader, is to be very wary of any part of the Establishment in that when they tell you something, it is important to question their logic and ethics (and lack thereof). Begin to ask yourself, 'What plot does their nefarious agenda march to?'

Larry provides his cartoons to a range of publications. His arms are wide and open in receiving your requests!

ACKNOWLEDGMENTS

To my most beautiful babe, Yoshie -- you are my everything, and my heart sings at the highest octave with you in my life. I bow to the Universe with immense gratitude that karma allowed us to be together in this lifetime. You are my deepest love. In allowing our hearts to beat as one, you have been instrumental in enabling me to provide this literary message to the Universe.

Skye – my soul-traveler from Sirius, I am immeasurably thankful for your choosing me as your Daddy. Follow the Path and all signals from the Universe to be everything you can as a leader for the 2029 event which is so important for so many. I love you SO much: you are my big boy hero!

Gaia – my precious princess from Pleiades, thanks for always coming down to Daddy's office and saying, "Good luck, Dada! Peace, White Light and Energy!" You kept me going. I love you more than all the stars in this universe and the ones bordering!

Sherpa and Yanpa: your top-dog loves you so much. Thanks for all the toe licks and support in the quietest hours of writing. You all gave me super-dog energy when I most needed it! And to Zo, Totoro and Tenzing: in finding you new homes in MT, NY and OR with new family, thank you for knowing what I had to do was very difficult for my heart; I will always miss you, but I know you are in good hands now. Toumae & Moro: we love any spiritual visitations, for memories of you both live on with joy.

Miguel Sanchez -- my dearest buddy of 26 years -- who I'd trust to take care of my wife on a camping expedition (well, maybe not, ha ha) … you are the person that always has understood my deepest sense of be-ing, sense of humor, dreams and goals of which has always provided a very special feeling throughout the years that is inseparable for lifetimes.

Katmandu Mehico -- to the incredible amount of gratefulness for being my brutha', my computer expert and my companion on trips worldwide. Remember that everyone has a little nook in them. I am so proud of you, for what you have accomplished!

Ev -- because your intelligence astounds me, may some of these thoughts allow you to escape the limitations that others place on you so you may maximize the Abundance.

Dan & Maarit (and family) – I love you guys. I always think of you. You are never far despite our geographical separation.

G-man, Big O -- it is my hope that these humble passages will in some way allow you to expand your lives in many positive directions. I look forward to getting even closer in years coming.

Dad – in 1980, you made a decision that was pivotal in allowing me to discover an acceptable reality, peace and pure joy. You believed in me when it was important, and no matter what words have been spoken, I send you love energy. May the rest of your Path be peaceful and joyful – for remember – we have a choice.

Mama – ganbare ne! I love you. Thanks for all your laughs! Steve – I know you may not agree with much of this book, but at least I appreciate your stance on agreeing to disagree. May truth be shown to you in good time and may your health be good.

Kelli the KK -- as my energetic companion I have a lot of affection for our deep friendship. You are a treasure in my life.

C -- to the deepest oceans and highest mountains, I appreciate your vibration and existence in my life. As my older 'sis', I truly adore you, and I send you the strongest energy I know how.

D-bone -- I am so obliged for your entering my life. You have the ability to help get this book to so many ... and I look forward to the evolution of just making it happen, diue! Don't forget to listen often to the song, "I Believe I Can Fly"!

Jules – dearest TF, to all future work together ... I marvel at all our communication through the Divine. It is a connection that I wouldn't give up for the world.

Mayline – you are such a beautiful spirit. I infinitely treasure your energy. I am always happy to be in your presence. Hugs forever for healing my energetic wounds.

Pickles and his goddess – the Constable raises his fingertips to yours and says, 'May all my energies be yours, and may all your weapons be integrated together so as to be one with One'.

AG master -- over the years, I have always looked forward to discussing different ideas with you. With utmost recognition to our buddy-ship, I am gratified for your believing in my Path.

To my "mothballs" lady – you helped me heal and for that I energetically love you. If it wasn't for your gentle goading, this book might not have been published until 2020. Hopefully one day I can pay your power bill for all your help and insights.

Mems -- reach out and grab the world with your smile, hard work and treating others with benevolent thoughts ... your unfolding gives me great hope! Thanks for our friendship.

Tim -- everything you want is out there. Thanks for our friendship that allows us to share much about life experiences.

Teens the Weens -- thanks for giving that "extra" organization and true caring to my family. Your help, especially at low moments, will always be cherished. You are such a great soul. Never forget baby steps, and one day you can fly, fly away.

Richie Rich -- for teaching me so much about life, especially the 'side' you have experienced. You're my older brutha' and I wear that badge with pride. Here's to that future radio show we'll do one day! I believe in you ... never forget that.

And the Pand -- I send you generous amounts of love. I smile so radiantly when I think of the wonderful gem of expression you are. I could hug you for days on end.

Darielle & Gary – with love for the graciousness of your energetically adopting me. Thanks so much for sending me the Ho'oponopono prayer, fixing the Little Blue Whale, emanating heart energy in healing sessions, and guiding me at times when I have sought refuge on darker days & at times of uncertainty. Ariana & Mark – always remember we are global sentient be-ings without borders; the new land you are on is safe.

e the Fidge – I hold many blessed memories of days and nights full of spiritual advancement – & I pour out my gratitude to you.

To the Squire, my "father accountant" and Jeralyn – I will always remember your gift of Abundance in Chappaqua. Thanks for everything over the years, and for believing in me.

Carla, Maca, the big JP and Ethan – a thousand arms of thanks for everything you have done to allow me to sip from the cup of and dance in the wonderfully higher vibration of a new land.

Fred – we attack! Your 'hideaway' in finishing this book was a true blessing. Thank you for your fatherly nourishment! And to you, Silvia, your beauty and poetic abundance shine a wonderful light on the world, especially to those that you hold and cherish.

Mae – I am so glad our paths hooked-up; I have truly welcomed your wisdom over the years. May all be well in your journey.

To the new father of Totoro: I look forward to good journeys down the road, and seeing you "down south". For helping me better communicate through technology for almost two decades, you have my utmost thanks. Don't forget that "business trip"!

Sal – I wish you much love in all learning and yearning to be the best person you can be in those circles you influence. Despite being "chalk and cheese", my brotherly love is still there.

Colette – I trust that the 'medicine' in this book will provide you a great boost in life – one that I know will empower you!

Rivka, Karah & Joe – I am proud to have you guys 'aboard' the "Skyaia Ship". Thanks for all the expertise you bring to this journey! To all you have done in social marketing, I am indebted.

Kelly – you taught me so much about spiritual connections in just one day. Gratitude for that special time eagle-watching.

To SDM, AZ Mom, and TN Mom – you have been and always will be a truly cherished energetic part of me. I am truly blessed to have so much maternal love and such a strong force for me.

To my shamanic healer, Stevi. Gratitude for touching me, my energy field and my life force. May the Cobra always be in peace.

Danyelle, Janet and all friends associated with Lhatong – it's been great to see your growth! Thanks for your support and friendship in vouching for my goals. I wish you Abundance!

Lori, your sweat lodge ceremonies have been unforgettable experiences that I shall treasure forever.

Kathy the KK and Jen the Ten – your path of discovery has also shown me so much. Your presence and your dedication to healing gives me many smiles; I warmly cherish your wisdom.

Olavo, mi maestro de Tai Chi y amigo verdedero: muchas gracias de todas las cosas positivas que me enseñas, incluyendo el hecho que toda la energía en el universo está connectada.

Val -- with all good intentions and energy from and to each other, you helped me in ways you may not know.

Christina – you know you are an energetic sister in Uruguay, and I value our new connection in many conversations forward.

Don – a big hug in remembering the day we flew the flag, and all those cups of tea out on the deck and on the driveway – all cherished memories. Thanks for helping me fight the darkness.

To my 'shipping team' in two hemispheres – I so much appreciate not only you protecting us in the big move, but also taking care of others that follow our path southward.

To all my very special clients -- you have my strongest handshake in thanking you so heartily for believing in me and my work in Planetary Threat Management as I strive forward in many different ways to give you an 'edge' with my unending commitment. Thanks for all your support to AFC.

To two special gurus – Dr. Wayne Dyer and Louise Hay – you have given me so much Light for many years – and I am enamored by your resplendent energy for moving humanity forward in such positive ways.

To Guzman, and all new friends in Uruguay (you know who you are): it is a true blessing that you have stepped into my life, and I look forward to all future healing, philosophical conversations, Tai Chi in the sun, and much more.

To all those that have worked with me in my career -- when I roll back the years, you have been instrumental. I know you have entered my life for a very specific reason, and I am so thankful.

To all so-called "controversial" scientists (in climate and health, and everything in between), allopathic physicians that truly do care and live for positive change, natural health doctors / practitioners / advocates worldwide, positive multi-dimensional travelers, peaceful mavericks, Mike Adams, James Gilliland, Dr. Joseph Mercola, Drunvalo Melchizedek, and so many other leaders: your talent and incredible words and ideas have helped shaped my thoughts and direction in life. Thank you so much for all you do on and for this blue planet!

Dottore Ek -- for all your valuable advice throughout the years, I am truly grateful despite some splitting of atoms over this and that.

When you close your Earth Walk, know that from now until then, and even after, I will bid you good energy.

Preston -- may all know of your moving film on Leonard Peltier -- I'm commanding the Universe for it to be well-known. Kris – I adore the strength you carry: thanks for our friendship.

Laura Harvey -- without your positive stream of energetic vibration, I know this book would not have looked as good.

Larry – your cartoons are a terrific part of this book, and I couldn't be more grateful to you for this part of the project. You bring laughter into a lot of people's lives … a precious gift.

To my birth mother – you indirectly taught me that the difference between the Path of Light and Dark is only a hair-width apart. Thank you! As we continue our journeys, may you experience many good rays on your sunrises ahead.

To all those people in my life that are from previous lives: some of you know who you are … I cherish our bond through time (otherwise known as intention).

To all new friends and contacts in the alternative media through radio, TV, print and other alternative means that have assisted in spreading the messages of Skyaia®, a tremendous thank YOU.

To those few that sued me through transgressions of hatred: one day you will realize how everything is all connected. I send you blessings of forgiveness for you were clearly misdirected.

To my nemeses, known and unknown, loud and mute: fear not,

that even though my light shines strong in your world of darkness, there is always room for you to enter once you energetically turn toward the Light of One.

Many thanks to all those that bought this book ahead of the publish date. Despite all the delays, you 'hung tough' with me, and I so much appreciate that strength and patience of a saint that you exhibited.

To all you amazing readers that have sought out this book (or it has sought out you) and avid believers in the incredible world of energy ... I vibrationally send you much abundance into your life, trusting that you can forward the message, tell about Skyaia®, and gain insights into what our lives are really, truly about.

My brain has probably elapsed in not mentioning some of you out there, but energetically I have never forgotten you.

And lastly, to all those that remain anonymous, in this dimension and others, from all origins – my immense gratitude for anything positive you have ever given me and continue to give our Earth. Without your energy, I could not intention to move the planet forward in a positive way. And to that, I hereby promise that I will never neglect or misuse the gifts you have given and continue to bestow upon me.

"This we know: the earth does not belong to [us], [we] belong to the earth. All things are connected like the blood that unites us all. [We] did not weave the web of life, [we] are merely a strand in it. Whatever [we] do to the web, [we] do to [ourselves]."

One version of a fragment of a speech given by Chief Seattle in December 1854, translated from Lushootseed, his native language; modern substitution of "us/we/ourselves" from the original "man/he/himself" respectively.

❖

"All truth passes through three stages. First, it is ridiculed. Second, it is violently opposed. Third, it is accepted as being self-evident."

Arthur Schopenhauer, German philosopher (1788 - 1860)

"If you spend your whole life waiting for the storm, you'll never enjoy the sunshine."

Morris West (1916 - 1999)

"I Have Sworn upon the Altar of God ... Eternal Hostility against every form of Tyranny over the mind of man."

Thomas Jefferson; September 23, 1800

Part 1
Transform Self

Preface
Access To The Last Frontier, Our Mind, Is Not Too Far Away

Climate change. Healing. Solar flares. Galactic shifts. Alien life. Mind control technologies. Commanding abundance. Energetic health. Life after death. The Establishment control.

These may at first seem like scattered thoughts, but they are all a part of our lives, whether we realize it or not. They are all about different energies, yet all these subjects are connected.

There are a myriad of connections between the cosmos and our cells: everything is happening in exact, precise sequence probabilities, no matter how low, and is all interconnected back to a Divine Source.

This is not about religion. This is not about revelation. This is not about war or peace.

This is about the triangular conjunction of electromagnetic science, multi-dimensional spirituality, and vibrational synergy.

This mystical yet mathematical Flow is Skyaia®. And this is not just about your Path, but it moreover the importance of our Journey together … not just in this dimension, but through other dimensions.

Until recently, I had no idea what series of events at the cosmic and societal level are beginning to unfold. It is something I think that will probably be on the order of mind-dazzling incredible. But there are impediments. There will be chaos. Yet when you are "in the know" you have a sharp 'edge'. And remember at least two things: never any fear, and, there are choices, individually and collectively.

When you read this book straight through, you will understand what is needed of you, and what you can expect in return. Begin by empowering yourself with knowledge. It is time to buck away from what the Establishment tells you, because clearly, many more are beginning to see the light – the vibrational force away from the psychotronic weaponry being used on too many of us.

Because every conscious entity from the cosmos to our cells is energetically connected Skyaia® covers so many topics: it does not have all the answers, but it certainly will open new lines of thinking enabling us to better understand the upcoming changes and the needs required of us.

Let us begin.

Chapter 1
Skyaia® Theory
New Thinking: Cosmic Change & Health Impacts

"WITH MY DEGREE IN *LAW* AND IN *PHYSICS* I HOPE TO CREATE A *REASONABLE DOUBT*."

Many will welcome the new ideas in this book and the theme that humanity must press forward in the name of freedom harder now that at any other time in history. Of course, there will be critics that say this book covers too many topics and is therefore disjointed, or they will say it is too esoteric or talks nonsense, or they will use any number of criticizing words, names or sentences to describe these contents. Some will tell you not to read it – afraid that you will 'wake-up'. In essence, they are terrified you will learn the truth, and that you will find out so much is hidden from us. They are fearful of you learning the legitimacy of the true origins of human be-ings is from the stars, or that chemo-'therapy' is actually a death sentence for cancer (which is a dis-ease mainly due to a disconnect of your electromagnetic body to Source). I will ask the critics to tell me why the Establishment wants you and I controlled, voiceless, and unable to achieve our true energetic freedom, and after that, then I will respond.

This is *Volume 1: Control or Freedom?*, and grounds us all in the same wavelength of how energy connects everything, details our purpose, and describes in detail the threats that we have to conquer. There is hope … in fact, I have a lot of it, despite the rather bleak situation of our news each day and the rapid degradation of the value system within many societies.

All things mentioned are connected, in more ways than in just the basic three-dimensional field, and therefore, it would be incomplete not to mention many interconnecting subjects in this book. In fact, if I'm guilty at something, this book borders more on potentially being unfinished than unfathomable. Ironically at that, there is no room for many things I wanted to include, but those will be covered in another part of Skyaia® in the future (make sure to read the Epilogue).

Magnetize Yourself Back To The Creation You Are A Part

There is an incredible number of connections between the cosmos and our cells. Our origins are not from Planet Earth. So much of the Truth has been hidden from us. But we are Awakening, and we are each are realizing we are a part of something much bigger. That is where I put a lot of my hope.

You may or may not realize that each of us can 'magnetize' the right people, things, conditions, health and so much more just by and from the way we think.

But sadly, so many of us have 'lost our way'. We have lost the purpose of life, we have lost how to be joyful, we have lost the feeling of togetherness, and we have lost the ability to be self-sustainable.

Instead, too many of us are angry, depressed, exhausted and a host of other negative emotions which deprive us of our given rights to magnetize our spiritual energy back to the Creative Source.

Our goal in life is to understand and then set course on a path to achieving the energetic vibration of equilibrium that is represented in Skyaia®.

Skyaia® represents:
1. everything in existence in our Sky, yet above and within the stars, the cosmos, the plethora of light, all realms and dimensions beyond,

2. everything in existence on, below and inside (within) our planet we so fondly call Mother Earth, or Gaia, and,

3. everything in existence in between including everything in all living things down to cellular, energetic and multi-dimensional levels.

As spiritual entities, we come from Sky (capital 'S'). Sky is the cosmos, Source or One. There is an exceptional amount of evidence that the very seeds of our existence come from Sky. That accumulation of proof has been largely shut-out to us. The reality on the construction, positioning and meaning of the pyramids, Stonehenge, and dozens of other sacred (aka sacred not only meaning 'religious' or 'spiritual' but also as 'access points to other dimensions') sights is just the beginning of a whole new world of knowledge that has been re-told and 'planted' repetitively as something else. Instead we have been brainwashed by fabricated stories that we kill for to believe in. Once we become open to Source, and it simply begins by speaking out loud the words, "I am ready to begin accepting all new ideas that I need to grow by tapping into Source," then energetically the abundance in your life begins to change.

WHAT IS SKYAIA®?

Skyaia® = Sky + Gaia.

Skyaia® says that all matter in the universe, visible or invisible, in any form, is integrated and weaved together via a complex network of mathematical intelligence that is electromagnetically and divinely connected.

Skyaia® is the energetic interconnectedness of science, climate, cosmic change, mathematics, advanced technology, natural health, alternative medicine, and spirituality, based upon the field of electromagnetics, with the purpose for individuals to achieve a higher awareness.

Skyaia® is the music of, in and throughout the Universe, connecting us, as be-ings of energy, to its ever-loving expanse. Tapping into Skyaia® is how to make your life full of Abundance. Being with Skyaia® means empowering yourself to think independently to maximize your 'star' of health (of five different points), and avoiding the corruption, deception, lies and energetic slavery of the Establishment that is NOT connected to the intelligence of Skyaia®. That is what this book is all about.

Now I just said a volume in a few pages. Forget 'out of the box': that is 'old hat' now. The new mode of thinking is multi-dimensional or even inter-dimensional.

Do you want an 'edge' in life? Of course you do. Well, without mixing words, it is essential to better understand energy. To be more precise, electromagnetic energy. From the inner workings of your cells to the huge reactions of the cosmos, electromagnetic energy and its many different variations and formats – originating many tiers up from a Divine State of harmonic sound and vibration – is what allows you and me to better understand the Universe and its beautifully clever functioning.

The electromagnetic energy imbued in a colony of ants walking across your driveway, or the multitude of possibilities of your unplanned day ahead, or the variation of heat expunged from a coronal mass ejection of the sun is not chaotic nor confused in any way; instead, all examples are intelligently designed through laws, cycles, continuity, intentions, affirmations, mantras, mathematics, prose and even a sense of humor.

Because of this Universal divine order, of which we are connected, we are guided by its energetic laws, but only if we choose to be. In other words, we all are "given" the keys to unlock the doors to the purest of manifestations, namely joy, inner freedom, the ability to express gratitude, and many more; but, it is our choice whether we use the keys to go to the 'other side', away from control, manipulation, negativity and so forth.

This Universal path of connections and doorways is not a 'program', because that word has the connotation of 'doing something without freedom or desire'. Instead these laws can be essentially split into four "commonalities" of which I call "The Four C's".

THE FOUR C'S

Your most important goals with everything from your cells to the cosmos are the four "C's":

1. Connect
    … as in, plug-in at a higher wavelength,
2. Communicate
    … as in, talk from and listen with your mind and heart to your Higher Self,
3. Collaborate
    … as in, pool resources with like-minded individuals to grow together and amass strength as a pod -- like a whale pod, and
4. Cooperate
    … as in, work efficiently as a team to a higher purpose in a peaceful manner

What most governments do – especially those that have The Agenda (more on this later) as their main goal -- in advocating war instead of peace, in turning a blind eye to toxins in our food and water instead of showing us how to be healthy, and in telling us that carbon dioxide is the root of all global climate change instead of telling us the truth about magnetic solar cycles that are highly correlated to temperature patterns -- is all against the grain of these 4 "C's".

The bottom line is this: the institutions that are hell-bent on control, the eugenicists and other 'dark matter' individuals (aka Luciferian-praising zealots, in a religious sense) do not want you or I knowing about Skyaia®.

THE FIVE 'STAR' POINTS OF OUR HEALTH

When we think of health, most of the time we think elements of physical health such as cholesterol level, fitness, the food we eat, the vitamins we take and so forth. But in the course of any twenty-four period, there are also other important parts: emotional health, mental health and spiritual health. Then there is the fifth segment (making the five points of a star shape): energetic or electromagnetic health. And that has four additional circles: individual energetic health / community energetic health / global energetic health/ and cosmic energetic health.

For optimal well-being, energetic health is the most important, period. Let me give you this analogy: your physical, emotional and mental health is your home. Your spiritual health is the satellite dish on your home's roof. And your energetic health is the very high, locking and electric-shock gate around your home. If someone tries to get into your home, and does so successfully, it means that your energetic health, the gate, was weak. (Aside, I know what some of you are thinking here: our abode can now be attacked from above by one of those government 'pets' -- the drone: it's still the same – energetic health is the force-field all around you, above you and below you).

Some people smoke for fifty years and don't get cancer. I am strongly against everything about smoking, especially the corporations that make such terrible things. But those that don't get cancer from smoking is because their 'protective gate', their energetic auric shield of health, is not punctuated (does not have 'holes' in it). And so an intruder, say the fungus or electromagnetic 'corruption' (altered form of energy) we know as cancer, cannot penetrate, thereby allowing the vibration of the cells to resist an attack and stay guarded from negative forces.

> Let me state something very important based upon energetic health: even though many other aspects of health are important in your overall spectrum of well-being, if you alter your energetic realm to positive – namely, affirmative, compassionate, cooperative, benevolent and one of appreciating of Self with gratitude for all in your life (even your challenges because they provide you with valuable lessons), you severely decrease your probability of getting cancer (and other serious debilitating dis-ease).

Here are some other matters that are important to share related to the composition of Skyaia® Theory, with a foundation of the Golden "Phi" Ratio and Fibonacci codes:

- Divine intelligence is creative, multi-dimensional, humorous, mathematical, structural, coded and connecting

- All living cells and matter in the cosmos replicate (and slough-off) with the same energetic signature, just in different frequencies and intensities; that is, the structural replication and sequential process of energy formation is similar throughout the universe

- There is a constant cycle of life and death: since energy is never created or destroyed, the vibrational signature of any life-force is eternal., including us as spiritual be-ings having a human experience

- The most powerful and free energy generated by the Universe is magnetic and multi-dimensional (aside: past races that lived on Earth – other extraterrestrial entities [see chapters on this] – left us pieces of the code to replicate this wonderful energy that is free for all, but the Establishment has kept it hidden)

- Gravity only exists in a 3-dimensional plane. Levitation is common in magnetic-based technology and is common in any 4+ dimensional field (aside: NASA and other parts of the Establishment are very careful not to reveal a lot of pictures of space voyages because they show orbs – other entities that exist that they don't want you and I knowing about; in the past, of course, they have made "mistakes" which have made others question)

- Bigger changes in energetic systems on Earth and with the sun cause large leaps in discovery, innovation, detections and inventions, as well as shifts in science, medicine, financial systems and health

- Changes in the energy of our sun and earth cause shifts or a transformation in our consciousness

- Once we harness the powerful magnetic centers on Earth, and triangulate in mathematical sequences, then unlimited energy generation exists.

THE FINGERPRINT OF DIVINE INTELLIGENCE

Does a change in cosmic energy affect a regional population's fertility rate? You bet -- sometimes increasing it, sometimes decreasing it. It's all cycles. And yet here is the important thing to remember ...

When we reach the understanding that there is a 'fingerprint' of Divine Intelligence in everything living, proven and confirmed by mathematical expression, and we can empower ourselves in understanding how this all works, AND we keep an open mind to inter-dimensional realities, then we can become more peaceful, have more joy, and generally-speaking, attain a higher level of Abundance in so many ways. We are then more often than not able to help others, be more compassionate, live a spiritually-guided life, be healthier at all levels (previously described in general terms), and see life not as a tough 70-100 year walk-around-the-track, but instead as a journey of growth, new aspirations, and making our planet better when we move on compared to feeling fortunate enough to be born here. You are here for a reason. Know it by commanding the Universe to show you (in dreams, by unlocking your God-given right to unlock your true potential). Get into the golden light of Skyaia®, and recognize that you -- as a divine part of Light -- can achieve so much more once you give-up your designed attachment to the Establishment. Join hundreds and thousands each day that are becoming Free energetic be-ings.

I am humbled to take you on a new journey in this book that will cover so many things, all related to each other in the big scheme of the meaning of life.

Chapter 2

Connected Beyond Our Dreams

Forget Your Past Indoctrination, Command Prosperity In The Now

The Universe Is A Mirror To The Thoughts & Emotions We Project

There is a new vibration. We have just entered a new era. This new energy is shifting our climate, our health, and everything in between. In fact, what is changing is the health of our climate and the climate of our health. And I would be lying to you if I told you things are moving toward the better. Ultimately, a change to the change is essential. It requires new thinking. There is a transformation, and if you have felt something new you are not alone; in fact, you are one of millions feeling the shift. The connectivity to millions of others will be explosive as the planetary electromagnetic pulse increases in strength, volatility and imbalance.

This vibrational shift is not just in this dimension: it overlaps into multiple dimensions, and at various times, the energy is intense. Often when this occurs, we "inexplicably" become very tired and/or depressed, or we feel aggressive like we are some kind of superhero. With more and more humans, with separation of the Fukushima radiation aside, it is increasingly likely that you experiencing a new illness, or negative health symptoms, especially if those energies wane and wax inside you. Furthermore, what it could be is something I call multi-dimensional inertia. Throughout the book, I will describe multiple dimensions (and inter-dimensional transference) more.

Everything is connected energetically, like the interactivity of a massive number of spider webs all being plucked by the Universe. I play by two rules: first, never break the spider's web you are in, or any other spider web: it's not 'if' but when you will need to be in another web to continue a stream of abundance; if you break it, your abundance could end. And second, symbolically, if you're a moth and you see a fly get caught in a strand along the way, stop and help ... don't just think because it's a fly and you are not then that is the excuse not to help. Compassion is the cushion you will need in a time of potential collapse. And at the times of tough going in your life, collapse is possible at any moment, but when you are compassionate, you will have at least a cushioned landing and attract higher energy.

WE ARE ALL CONNECTED THROUGH THE PLANETARY ELECTROMAGNETIC PULSE

This book is all about energetics – and the incredible realization that we are all connected. But it goes a lot further like I said in the preface (in case you missed those important words in possibly one of the most important parts of this book). It smashes down on the corruption and lies that exist in climate science. It exposes the corruption and lies of mainstream health.

I used to be very angry about the illusionists, the Satanists and the con artists of the world. These are the entities (people and organizations) that hide behind their camp lines strategizing on how they can tax us more, swindle us more, make us unhealthier, ruin the planet, and change our energetic switchboards to control us more.

The anger only hurt me. So I had to change. In this book, I share with you how I did that. If you are angry now, you can cleanse and turn the tide like I did. We can still vent the anger, but not allow it to consume us or others. And we can still change the world positively by channeling the energy of anger into the energy of passion in achieving positive change.

We must each realize that the body can heal itself without the use of Big Pharma toxic drugs and chemicals. We must stop the lies that big corporations trounce upon us.

The so-called Establishment are those that wish to perpetrate lies regarding natural health, dis-ease, medicine, climate science, space threats, technology, finance, our origins, our true potential – cerebrally, and everything in between with the purpose of minimizing access of the truth to us, the underprivileged majority, what they call the 'peasants' of the world.

The elite in society, which are usually below but can be a part of, the so-called Bilderbergs, Illuminati, Committee of 300, Council of Foreign Relations (CFR) and other front groups, actually consist of multiple tiers of slaves that nefariously work in many sinister ways together. This is no conspiracy theory: in doing extensive research, it is what you will discover too, and it will become more obvious when you command an opening of your Eye (aka, your Third Eye or connection to Universal Knowledge). In society, the elite include the higher 'rungs' of some of the corporate 'topdogs'. This includes, in the world of health and food, bike-pedaling management under the lashes and tremendous toxicity of the owners of Monsanto, the Federal Drug Administration (FDA), Merck and many others. (Side note: you only need to read the August 15, 2011 issue of Fortune magazine to realize the toxicity of a drug company). And in the world of climate science, there are many that don't have a scruff of intelligence between their eyeballs other than to parrot-fashion copy mistruths, like so many themes spouted by liberal media, the Bill and Melinda Gates Foundation [which shows how someone can jump ship from computers to exude a newly-found 'expertise' (not!) in climate science, while all at the same time pushing the sick world of eugenics], the United Nations' IPCC and many others. And by the way, just look it up: the Bill Gates Foundation is developing bracelets that track mental and emotional responses such that these devices will be used against you in the future; essentially, it is a compliance technology to monitor you. Once you start digging you will see the real objectives of these cabals.

This Book Is About New Thinking & A Choice For Humanity

This book is about making change in Self through positive affirmations, through grasping the ability to fulfill one's existence, dreams, goals and joy by attaining a stream of positive energy for a brighter future. I am talking about empowering your Self to a new level using your greatest asset – your mind – so that you can prosper, gain an advantage and otherwise go up against those that try to proliferate against you fortified with intelligence, knowledge and mental will. Know when I say this I am not campaigning for any violence. I come in peace -- harmony to change things at a consciousness level for positive outcomes.

This book is about dismantling the doomsday scenarios in your life. The Universe is SO intelligent that all you have to do is think AND believe in Abundance that you start attracting it to you. Any future of Armageddon, portrayed by the Establishment, that is wrapped around you to the point of suffocation so that you reek of fear, is the wrong path in life.

This book is about unlocking the keys to gain personal freedom, to bringing back ancient memories of how you can heal yourself, to choosing wisely on where you decide to live, and how you can learn how to protect yourself from the manipulated and weaved lies that are promulgated by the Establishment.

This book is about cosmic energies, in explaining who we are as human beings, in understanding the origins of our seed of life, and our ultimate challenge as a global population.

Finally, this book is all about a choice for humanity. We can either:

1. Move into the Light, learn to cooperate and be at peace with each other, become self-empowered and learn to think for ourselves, rather than live hand-to-mouth and rely on Establishment entities, or
2. Remain in the Dark, and slip deeper into it toward a mass enslavement of mental control, a fascist state of existence, an unquestioning soul-less bunch of infertile animals raised by elitist Luciferian 'farmers' who shock us into human corrals

I know I unquestionably want "option one". I command the first choice, and nothing but it. And so it is. I know a ton of people that want choice one.

Unfortunately, there are quite a few souls out there that have given up or are giving up, and are falling into the meat grinder of the Establishment, option two. Through your persistence, you can help them, if you know of a soul like this. And you CAN help yourself if you feel as though you are slipping into that blade.

And I implore you that if you feel dull, or beaten down, or not excited to seize the moment in this very important juncture in our evolution, then you must read this book and know that it is critical you see your important role in the coming years ahead.

Using a computerized analogy, many don't know how to configure and defragment their hard drive. It is okay to keep growing your hard drive, but we must maintain it all and never make the ultimate flaw – allowing a virus or another host to control us internally! And by the way, never take the 'mark of the Beast' by getting any tracking device medically put into you ... ever.

Climate and health are perhaps two of the biggest and most important subjects in the world. About eighty-five percent of news stories are directly or indirectly related to climate and health.

Climate and health affect us all. Climate change is everything not only above us, but is everything below our feet – earthquakes, volcanoes, tsunamis, methane burps and much more. Health is everything inside us as much as the air, food, water, soil and plant life around us.

So if you and I are being given a very small percentage of the real science and the real medicine that is taking place in the world,

and lied to ninety percent of the time, that is a lot of your life and my life that is going down the wrong path. It is time to get on a bandwagon that corrects this. But again, I always say any change must come through a new type of arsenal: collective mental energy that creates positive choices and new ideas, never physical violence or negative intention (both of which ultimately hurt your energy / Self).

Once you tap into the power of the human mind and access it for positive change, you will quickly understand why transformation enacted by physical altercation is negative and minuscule in its comparative role for bringing about a safer, more positive world for us, our children, our grandchildren and beyond.

Now the whole mental power topic may seem like a concept that has no meaning to you, or it may have meaning but it may not be well understood how it can give you a personal advantage. Let me be blunt: the future, starting from this moment, is all about your mind, my mind, the mind of your next door neighbor, the mind of the guy who lives in Nepal, the mind of the ten-year-old girl growing up in Kazakhstan, and the mind of the military leader that has a life-altering moment – all in which a new light bulb turns on inside your head – and starts allowing you to have a two-way communication with a Divine Intelligence, a power source that is so incredible, so trustworthy, so beautiful, that it begins to shift your life to one of abundance and prosperity. And from there, your energy vibration shifts, and it spreads outward in a ripple-like fashion to all those around. And like the multiplication of doubling a penny every day for thirty days and getting over a million dollars, so too will the positive energy spread around the globe, until we get to a point of Oneness, with a goal of global nurturing instead of global war, a goal of global altruism instead of global selfishness, and a goal of global love rather than a goal of global hate.

Upcoming challenges we have coming are unique, profound, complex and serious. But in reality, when we learn to put our minds together, the risks of potential biblical proportions can be safely neutralized.

> Deactivation of the threat is our choice – it is the choice of humanity. Deactivation of the threat is done through the mind, not through physical violence. Once you learn how powerful your mind is, in connecting with other minds, you will be able to overcome any challenge.

But first, we must learn to live as One.

That means teaching our children from today onward to do and act in peaceful ways and means. It is imperative to show them that our thoughts as much as, if not more than, our actions, have energetic consequences. That is, everything that happens, everything that exists, whether it is a thunderstorm in Papua New Guinea, or a cancer cell in your cousin's aunt's lymph nodes, or an ant crawling across your front door step, or a mental plan of reciting answers to an job interview next week, all of these examples have a vibration, a wavelength, a frequency of energy. Your thoughts have and produce energetic consequences. The flood that happens next summer has repercussions of how high the heat may climb in the week following. The type of food and quality of water you consume will have an energetic effect – either positive or negative – on that cancerous node.

> Energy frequencies or vibrations can and will breed upon themselves because they will be reflected just like a mirror

back to its source. They will be attracted to energy of similarity or likeness, and they will gather more energy of their own type.

So, if you flick someone off in traffic and have a 10-minute period of road rage, you can bet close to one-hundred percent accuracy that at least the same but very likely a substantial amount more energy in like intensity will come back at you, sometimes immediately but more often with a delay.

If you get down on the floor and shut your eyes and kiss a dog's head (that you know and it knows you), other dogs will come over and start licking you in appreciation of your gesture of love. Like attracts like. That is why droughts continue on and on and on until some new energy 'breaks' the cycle. That is why flooding attracts more rainstorms. That is why when one member of a family gets cancer, another in the family is more likely to get cancer, especially if they live and interact together or nearby, because energetically, the cellular vibration is 'copying' and radiating outward through others' auric shells.

That is, since just about almost every human being has an aura – an energetic signature – that is even a higher and more advanced way of expressing individuality compared to the trillion plus or more differences between a set of fingerprints – it is known that if the circumference of my aura frequently touches and interacts with the aura of some other family person or co-habitant in the same space, then the vibration of both person's cells are going

to have similarities. That is, their immunity may become comparable. This is why a man and woman, or same sex loving couple, that have lived with each other together for so many years begin to "feel as one", or why some people express their emotions like their animals or vice versa.

There is so much for us to learn in energetic medicine, I am just offering the first spoon of honey for you to suck and savor. Energetic medicine is a very exciting future. We will leave behind the Stone-Age "health" practices of chemotherapy and other allopathic ways that treat the symptoms incorrectly – but not without a struggle – again one that must start with action from the mind – the "new" force of power in the near future behind changing things that are no longer wanted.

Cerebral Energetics

Certain groups of those with gifts of remote sensing or bilocation or telemetric clairvoyance will come together – not even physically – but in the collective mind – and will 'power-up' to change negative events, or even will / intent (as a verb) a certain negative result to cease. For example, people could will / intent the cessation of chemotherapy (which I will tell you right now is nothing more than an allopathic doctor-assisted form of euthanasia), and in the same period of group collusion of mental consciousness energy, they could command new, positive ways to cure cancer.

This of course may seem like a bunch of fantasy to those not willing to see multi-dimensional reality, but I will be blunt: we each have a choice in our own energetic futures.

> That's right – there is soon coming a change where evolutionary more and more human minds will be able to change events and occurrences for the positive or overall good through what I call "cerebral energetics".

You can climb aboard the train of positive affirmation, learning how to empower yourself and align your goals with the "New Age" of tapping into energetic intelligence, and knowing the truths on climate change, future cosmic interactions and how there are already other cosmic entities / energies here other than 'earthlings / humans'.

Or you can stubbornly grip onto the past, have the Establishment tell you when you can unzip, be in fear of lack of money, worry about this, that and the other instead of learning how to command prosperity into your life, and go out kicking and screaming all because you decided to sync-up with the energy of being controlled by those that didn't want you to become free.

You can change this periodic dark path of the new-type 21st-Centrury energetic slavery. I have journeyed full-circle and have been energized beyond using any extra-strength Duracell or Energizer battery. In this book, I will reveal so many things to you – many of which may stun you, or daze you, or shock you, but it will be a good thing to allow you to hear ways to unshackle you from the falsehoods you have learned in health and science, and put you back on your high horse so you can ride strong, and allow you to do the right things in positive light.

This book is nowhere near your average read about health. Nor is this anywhere near your average book on climate science. It fact, it purposefully deviates from Mainstream developments because there is so much in Mainstream that is not accurate, genuine or even reality. In other words, the libretto you are about to sink your teeth further into is totally against the fabrication, duplicity, the manufactured cock-and-bull stories, and all the sleaze associated with the Establishment, the Illuminati and those that think their behinds are made of gold and their stuff doesn't stink.

Essentially, while a portion of the most powerful and ill-intenting corporations, crooked Establishment agencies and wealthy individuals gone astray are setting course on an overall egotistical betrayal to the advancement of the human race, I am on a journey of reality, enlightenment and illumination, and I look forward to counting you in on my march to reality and legitimacy and overall freedom.

Why? Because we are at a critical juncture at this time to move off the train track from an increasingly worse socio-economic chaotic and bloody wreck to a totally different path, making a 180-degree switch toward expansion of individual empowerment, and debunking the swarm of lies that buzz around us by unshackling the chains that bind us, thereby allowing us to lead to greater fulfillment in self-progress toward a brighter future of innovation in health and science that is energetically positive.

So far I have just brushed upon many subjects from climate to health, our freedom and the goals of corporate and technological enslavement – but it is all energetically connected.

And now I will begin to explain so much more …

CHAPTER 3

No Ordinary Shift

This Time We Are Waking Up Faster Than Ever Before

"IT SAYS *NOT* TO USE HEAVY MACHINERY WHEN *TAKING* THESE. WHAT'S HEAVY *MACHINERY*?"

Things are really shifting now. The Awakening has not only begun in full swing, it is accelerating. You may not even know what you are feeling, but since you have this book in your hands, you have a fair to excellent grasp of knowing something vibrational is happening, more than your eyes are telling you.

The disinformation, the untruths and the manipulations of information in technology, science, our planet, medicine, the origins of humans, and so many subjects and fields of paramount importance is increasing. Fortunately, the tide is turning to the advantage of humanity on the subjects of health and climate -- two much related fields in coming years and decades ahead. Moreover, the awakening, the courage of others coming forward to express higher intelligence, new realizations rewriting humanity and so many advancements in making our lives more efficient are increasing. Of course, some weeks, however, it is hard to see this because those with messages of hate, deception and greed win over the cosmic bounty of goodness. The goal toward changing the negativity of the Establishment is gaining strength -- but in order to be successful, it must NOT be physical. As the Awakening continues, the People will discover their true strength in numbers through Cerebral Energetics -- the power of the mind and connection to each other's energetic vibration.

THE CLIMATE OF OUR HEALTHCARE & THE HEALTH OF OUR CLIMATE IS BECOMING SICKER

We have continued challenges in front of us. Now is a critical time. Let me focus on two very important areas. Both the climate of our healthcare and the health of our climate is becoming sicker. Reinforce the sickness with the lies, corruption, and just absolute and utter horse muck from so many double-talking mouths, and one must ask, is it any wonder why two of the most important subjects that affect all of us -- health and climate -- are deteriorating in quality and becoming fraudulent.

So many people are fed-up with allopathic medicine and its "here [schmuck], take a pill" mentality. Allopathic medicine shouldn't even be called medicine, especially since many of the side effects of Big Pharma's poisons and the damage done to the body and mind from them can be worse than the original ailments! If you have half a million in the bank (or want to indebt yourself for decades to come), if you have a big ego and trip out on power, if you get tired of listening for more than 5 minutes to people with ailments, then becoming your average allopathic doctor might be really a good career track for you.

I have to say at this juncture, that even though there are some allopathic doctors doing absolute wonders on our planet at this time, and that number is growing with time, most of them are full of ire or egotism. Many (I didn't say all) allopathic doctors relate to each other through their love for control and thinking their "back pantry doesn't stink after they empty it out". Excuse me, but unfortunately, it is necessary to be this crude because the majority like myself is sick to death of the increasing lack of doctors who truly care. So many (over 80%?) allopathic doctors have forgotten their Hippocratic Oath, and have an overall lack of willingness to care about healing. Nowadays, it is all about profit and peddling drugs for their bosses, the Big Pharma industry. And even if many of those doctors feel 'trapped', it is time they take a stand to fight the 'cancerous' corruption.

Let me switch gears for a second: people are also so fed-up with propped-up specialists that talk about global warming (what should be called natural or planetary or even cosmic climate change) as if they have been studying it their whole lives. What pray tell does Al Gore or Bill Gates know about climate change? I ask that because all of sudden they are the new spokesmen for reducing human-caused carbon-based climate change (and have many speeches by twisting in and advocating eugenics). Bill Gates should stick to computer systems (or perhaps just roll out of town due to the superiority of Apple's technology), and not use his vast hoard of money to corruptively dabble in lying "science" and eugenic de-population schemes. Oh yes, Mr. Gates is one big bad wolf alright.

WE MUST WAKE-UP, FASTER THAN EVER BEFORE

We are being deceived, conned and misinformed at an increasingly alarming rate. We are being swindled in the daytime and hoodwinked at night on scientific scams and health mistruths.

It is totally untrue that the longevity of the average person in the United States of America is going up. The truth is it is going down. With obesity, stress, medical errors, radiation in the atmosphere (from Fukushima especially now entering the Western USA region and other key States, and cancer rates all the highest they have ever been in modern history, it is a complete lie to say we are living more productive, longer lives. We are not. And yes, many studies in recent years are beginning to prove this by courageously running up against the Establishment.

If you are in the position to know something that can help others (and thereby help your own karmic journey and joy), and you have the information to show that the Establishment is lying, be brave, be a whistleblower, and show the People through peer-to-peer review (not the old-fashioned peer-reviewed process which is politically dominated by these lying sociopaths that wax on the polish of the black boots of the Establishment). Why do you think the controllers want to shut-down the Internet (or at least have regulations or laws saying that they can 'pull the plug' if and when they want to)? It's because they are afraid that the peer-to-peer review of scientific and health-related matters (showing the real causes of climate change, or that energetic medicine can cure cancer or Multiple Sclerosis and much more) will outshine their black magic with firm ties to the Occult.

In fact, with the average American sitting in front of their television on an average of 140 hours a month, the average person's metabolism is not only getting slower, thereby putting on the pounds, having more heart issues and seeing a quicker demise, but also their average intake of the all-important vitamin D3 is at an all-time low. Why is that important? Minimal vitamin D3 due to decreasing amounts of sunshine is leading to a depleted immune system, more illness, more dis-ease. And you guessed it, what is that leading to? More Big Pharma pills.

To see an amazing quick positive change: unplug your TV, take a daily walk, sleep just one hour more a day, read up on the benefits of taking 5,000 – 10,000 mg of vitamin D3, and you will, with over ninety-five percent confidence, have less illness and live a longer life. For some, that may not be that easy, but for most, it is that simple as just re-reading the beginning of this paragraph. And yet, the Establishment focuses on putting Mind Control Technologies (MCT's) in the latest TV's without you even knowing about it. Thanks to my dear friends at awakenvideo.org, just read-up on mnemonic circles / mind control if you want to go down a deep hole in uncovering he truth about the harm done to your brain by the 'elite forces'. The Establishment also comes out and says that you must avoid the sun because it is bad for you. It is simply not true. We'll get into the sun later on, but for now, know that approximately ninety percent of the froth that is spewed-out from the forked tongues of many in command are outright lies. Even though ten percent may have some accuracy, you'd be much better off to run the opposite way on much of the advisory disinformation that could and does eventually harm you either physically, mentally, emotionally, spiritually or energetically.

Shifts Are Becoming An Everyday Occurrence

The word 'shift' is becoming as ubiquitous as rain falling from darker clouds. There are shifts in the economy, shifts in global relationships (from corporate to friendship to family), shifts in science, shifts in medicine and shifts in even the way you eat, sleep, and breathe. This time though, these shifts are happening more frequently, and with increasing intensity and greater breadth. If you feel or sense many alterations, modifications, swings, adjustments, adaptations and just pure outright change are 'hitting' you – sometimes all at once – to the point where you feel it is overwhelming – then you have "logged-in" to this new era. And you may be feeling beleaguered and weighed-down -- literally 'snowed-under' by societal shift -- more now than at any other time in the past because you are sensing at least a fourth dimensional impact upon your electromagnetic aura.

There are so many changes happening all at once. So many of us are experiencing, sensing, undergoing and becoming increasingly aware of this disorder, upheaval and confusion in our lives. The frenetic pace is to the point where it is almost a rebellion of self-awareness.

Our Perception Of A New Planetary Movement Is In Fact A Revolution Of Consciousness

The usual connotation of the word 'revolution' is disruptive, but then we must remember there is the revolution of planet earth around our sun. In that sense, there is a 'turning', a movement of energy. As our blue sphere orbits our sun, almost all locations go through changing seasons on variations in temperature or moisture or both. When you think of your life, has there not been seasons and cycles too? Although there has likely been mishaps and challenges, growth provides wisdom, and that is positive. So while the initial thought of revolution might have been along the line of having to fight, war and complete mayhem, it only takes a few moments to use our collective insight in seeing there can be a positive connotation to a seemingly negative word.

The point here is that we all have a choice in the way we think, and there is no more important time than now to gear-up a new way of thinking, by choosing a positive track of living, and making decisions OUTSIDE of what the Establishment says. Some allopathic doctors and authorities will tell me I am being irresponsible, and they can have their First Amendment opinion expressed too. But hear me well: we are entering the largest shift that humanity has ever experienced, especially as we go through what I am calling the largest Establishment-caused global health disruption in the history of human beings, which is bigger than any Fourteenth Century Black Death (plague) or the spread of AIDS. When you add together the complete and utter disregard for human life by the Establishment by spending billions of dollars a day on military incursions and causing panic, fear and the smell of death, instead of putting just one-hundredth of that amount in figuring out a way to quickly fix the catastrophe of Fukushima and stop the release of radioactive plumes circulating the Northern Hemisphere week upon week upon week, it is an absolute abomination and a form of genocide by the ill ilk of these so-called leaders that tell everyone through Mainstream Media that they are doing everything they can. They are not and are clearly not. Solutions exist to fix this madness, but these psychopaths do not want to end the suffering. We must see that we are being brainwashed in so many ways, from the lithium and fluoride in our water (research and scientific papers prove that fluoride calcifies the pineal gland which then in effect closes the Third Eye, the gateway to Universal Knowledge), to the heavy metals sprayed in our air to the "soft" electromagnetic pulse weapons and/or psychotronic weaponry being used not only in natural storms to change the brain and health auric frequencies of local populations, but also to create natural events (like earthquakes, tsunamis, and even the holding back of dimensional shifts), and so much more.

The Establishment knows exactly what they are doing. The Establishment thinks they are more clever than the People. The Establishment thinks they can wield more power over the People through their drones and fear-mongering techniques, but ONCE we, the People, can begin UN-programming, and use our minds collectively to grab our power back to make the Establishment work for us (and not the other way around which has been the main cause of corrupting societies), then the planet will be safer and our health will improve. We will stop the absolute craziness of fascist-minded scientists that have been led astray by money and other ego-oriented prizes ... the same scientists at the Carnegie Institute of Science and other idiotic thinktanks that scream we need to put nano-sized particles or crystals in our skies to reflect sunlight to cool the planet. We will cease these zany geoengineering techniques of spraying our skies from white to blue with barium and aluminum which make our children's brains smaller.

PRIMP: You Can Begin Programming The Establishment (& Your Own Abundance) Today

Spoken words and thoughts are energy, and although we cannot see them, they have powerful abilities to change the course of our revolution – the revolution of our life around the Universe. You can begin today. Sit down quietly with your eyes closed. Imagine a politician that is doing sinister things like some of the ones I have mentioned already and have yet to describe to you. Then imagine you are talking with this person and you are saying exactly what you want to say. Believe that this has actually happened, and then command "And So It Is". Do this repetitively. And you watch the results after a few months: the technique is incredible because when many do the same thing, it changes the energetic proportions of actions to go toward the greater good of the majority. And since most people want what you want -- peace, love, health, joy, protection, prosperity and safety -- we can in effect turn around the direction of evil. This is not just some airy-fairy technique.

This is the power of prayer plus collective (united) consciousness shifting the vibration of an action. This is what I call 'People Ruling In Mind Power' (PRIMP). And that is how to derive everything from your own abundance to the wonderful changes for the planet. Of course, your actions must be in the greater good, and they cannot be ruled by ego (i.e., look what I did!), and you must be patient for it can take time to go into effect. But I will stress that Cerebral Energetics is the future, and I, for one, will grow this outward in many circles from this point forward.

Of course, the challenge we each have is to 'flick the switch' from interpreting and forwarding a negative to a positive. See or hear the word revolution and instead of thinking how to get even with the wrongs done against you, know instead that revolution can be a growth cycle that necessitates adaptation and ends with a positive outcome. Although it is not very obvious, and many would present a heated argument against the following, there is always a more positive meaning to just about anything, even some of the worst experiences in life. There are so many disruptive forces in motion at this time, likely affecting you, your friends, your family, even people down the road and on another continent that you either hardly know or have never met.

Cycles of change will always be upon us. Yet the ones about to occur are going to be highly energetic.

Being In-Tune With Higher Forces Gives You Strength

This shift is not just happening to us humans. It is happening to all living, sentient beings – ants, whales, robins – and trees, oceans, airmasses, sand particles, rocks and everything that has a presence. Sentient means not only conscious and living, but responsive and receptive. Of course, if we measure sand particles moving along a beach, there is an incredible philosophical wonderment that could be paralleled to our human lives: are they 'forced' by violent gusts of wind and harsh-crashing waves, or are they merely adapting … flowing … to the bigger forces in which they already "understand" that there is a greater purpose in movement and that 'fighting' for their so-called position on the beach is perhaps not only futile but also not for their higher good. This might be a truly outlandish personification of sand, but if each of us for a second represents one of these sand particles, the question becomes are you in-tune with these higher forces – the proverbial wind and wave actions, and are you open to change or are you resigned to not shifting? If you are open to shifting, and knowing it is for the greater good, then you will gain strength. If you cannot adapt to changes coming, for whatever reason, by especially if your ego is strong, then you will become weaker. It's that simple.

Everything has an energetic vibration. Everything has meaning. There are more energetic vibrations than ever before, a record number of interactions, and that is simply why our daily lives appear to be more intense.

There will always be greater forces that challenge us.

The Awakening is a shift that necessitates us all to see the multi-dimensional reality of our be-ing, of our breadth, of our journey, of our karmic path, and of the Universe. The proverbial 'waking up' can be a joyous experience: it is all about making it so. Yet it requires you to lean into the change, to adapt to the new, to live in love not in fear, and to help others. Joining energetic forces helps your neighbor, the woman or man in another land thousands of miles away, and you and your family.

Each of us has the choice to make the shift in joy each and every day. In the Constitution of the United States of America, it essentially says that we the People, have the power to make the change we desire. Let us take this very important document and apply its eloquence and wisdom in the 21st century by knowing that our thoughts are energetic potential actions waiting to be shifted to a kinetic state that can then shift experiences. Then we can apply those principles knowing that each individual truly can make a difference on a plane that more and more are understanding to be real: that of the electromagnetic realm. The same one that governs our immunity, our health, our joy, our abundance, the reactions around us, the climate, the planetary challenges and everything that is sentient and moving.

Yes, there will continue to be pulsations of energy that create challenging experiences for us not only as individuals but also as a collective enterprise. However, when we each can make a choice to think positively, and a huge number of thoughts and actions reach a critical positive mass, a chain reaction so strong can cause an immensely grand positive reaction. We each have the power to make a difference, and it all starts now with your next breath and your next thought.

CHAPTER 4

COSMIC CHANGE & HEALTH IMPACTS

How Our Bodies, Minds & Immunity Are Affected By Vibrational Changes: Seeing With Unclouded Eyes

As things, both small and large, come in front of us in our daily lives, there is always change. Larger challenges will present changes that most are not used to. But it's all for a reason: energy has to come and go, and sometimes the magnitude of it has to be large in order to shift other things. As you travel on your path, know that you are a part of the intricate web, and that when you ease into the change in front of you, the phase of acceptance-adaptation (the process I have termed that literally means you are ready to adapt because it is a part of one's journey) and the energy that comes from graciously accepting it will make it all the more joyful. That is, instead of concentrating on when and where, you will be able to enjoy the points of joy along the path.

Much of "modern" or Western aspects of health revolve around physical well-being. The allopathic world treats an issue in the liver separately to say the frequency of a headache, the color of one's hands, or even one's inability to conceive -- when all these things *could* be related. That is, much of Western medicine today does very little to concentrate on the human-being holistically. The American Medical Association (AMA) and other grievously erring, stubborn heavyweight institutes that are bloated with corrupt money streams (no apology here, I state things as I have researched them to be) continue to steer the American population down the wrong roads. Although some positive changes are being made, it is more fortunate that many more people are making the shift to realizing the holistic Self, sometimes courageously against their "main" doctor, and moving to holistic-centered forms of healing, which is then fueling the demand for more advanced methods to better health.

SHED YOUR SKIN TO BECOME RENEWED

This process is akin to a snake shedding its skin; and it is interesting to note that right before this period of renewal, a snake's eyes become cloudy and it cannot see very well. We humans are at that stage, where the AMA and other similar parasitic chameleon-like centers of dishonesty try to keep us in the dark; but, we are ready to shed, and so it will happen. When doctors and people from all walks of life discard our need to rely on the AMA (including MD's that have memberships), we will come out as a 'shiny' new entity. I remember as a kid going out looking for snakes and if I saw that they were really shiny, I wouldn't go near them because I knew that meant they were really alert and their eyesight was excellent.

Imagine if you could see multiple dimensions 'outside' and next to our own three-dimensional space. In the air there are "energy lines": they are wavy and connect points of like energy, and they are constantly moving. These connective formations create a vibrational field, and run the gamut from very positive to very negative. If you have ever gone somewhere and suddenly not liked the 'feeling' of being there, you could be detecting a field of pulsating energy that is literally weakening your cellular vibration. It feels uncomfortable because it is causing a deterioration in your electromagnetic field, which is thereby hurting your immunity. It is almost as if you feel a 'sting' by a hornet, but it is at the electrical and energetic wavelength -- kind of like having goosebumps because of an emotion that changes your neuro-circuitry. As human beings, we all have the ability to detect other vibrations, both good and bad, it's just that most people are not aware of what is going on. But now that we are waking-up to our holistic selves, thanks to Earth energies that are pushing us to see and feel more, our awakening in a multi-dimensional space is expanding, sometimes intensely for an increasing portion of the population.

THE AWAKENING IS HAPPENING DUE TO VIBRATIONAL SHIFTS

This awakening is happening because there are currently large vibrational shifts and more intense ones are coming. It would be too much if we received the sequence of a large shift all at once, so the benevolent Universe, with all its mathematical and divine intelligence, is gently but continuously prodding us to move forward. This is the leap of faith that we must make, or we face getting stuck in an old energy paradigm which would make us age quicker, become more depressed and overall cause us to 'dry-up' in a relatively short period of time like a peach in the hot sun.

Of course, the overwhelming number of doctors that are stuck in the old paradigm are going to say this is complete rubbish, and they will call me delusional and I'm sure much worse. Again, like I have said before, everyone is allowed their own opinion. However, I would like to add that much of this book is backed-up by scientific principles, you just have to dig deeper than the sources from which most get their information.

FOLLOW YOUR INTUITION, LITERALLY THE ENERGETIC DIMENSION OF YOUR FUTURE SELF

It is important that if you are feeling new sensations to expand or move, new feelings to grow and leave behind the old, and new emotions to spring forward and experience something new ... then DO it ... make the shift. Do not have fear that you are 'waking-up'. Your "voice" of Higher Self is one-hundred percent of the time entirely accurate and wishes only the best for you because it knows the superlative Path for your spirit and karma to follow.

CATASTROPHIC ERRORS IN ALLOPATHIC MEDICINE

The biggest irony is that within the next decade, possibly even just in the next five years, there will be such catastrophic errors in allopathic medicine, that the boom in holistic health will be absolutely huge. Already, medical errors causing long-term hardship in normal living, paralysis and many times a painful death, is on average the third cause of death in Western nations, especially in the USA. My prediction is that as people in the allopathic world are worked more (with grueling shifts sometimes lasting sixteen to even thirty-five hours with no sleep, especially becoming more common even amongst seasoned doctors as overall medical staff decrease in most cities), there will be much more of an increase in medical "mistakes". Maybe someone *really* famous (not just a Hollywood star) or even a president / prime minister will die of medical "incorrectness" (and of course it may take a few years for five juries and a long drawn-out court battle to prove it so) and that will be the catalyst to finally begin to shake some sense into this ongoing and increasing madness. But until then, expect the status quo with tens of thousands of people dying from the wrong tranquilizer, or a zombie nurse giving the wrong medicine to a certain person because s/he did not check the difference of two letters in two patients' names in the same ward. Medical errors account for such a huge death toll, but it is something that is just 'brushed under the carpet' by too many medical administrators.

As the natural energy vibrations expand on our planet, causing our intuition to grow and expand, the 'old' will be brought down and the 'new' will take its place. The goal is to reclaim our freedom and to stop the tyranny and fraud that is trying to get a hold on so many of us. It will be a fight, but I am optimistic that the ego-driven medical criminals of the world will be brought to Universal justice.

Meanwhile, there is fortunately a much more advanced track of medicine that emphasizes the holistic electromagnetic be-ing of the human, and realizes that our bodies are connected to our minds, and that our emotions are a huge part in our overall well-being and healing. Traumas, both emotional and physical, can already be healed by kinesiologists. Take that at least one level higher: there will soon be more countries (not likely the USA, sad to say) that allow healing to take place at the electromagnetic realm. Moreover, this superior path of holistic alternative medicine takes the time to understand a person's thoughts, past traumas, their physical environment, spiritual experiences and so much more. And because we are soon on the frontier of these "New Age" principles being accepted as the best paradigm, they will then be taught as 'standard' at a young age in school. Of course, the peer-to-peer review will be especially important because people will find an energy practitioner mainly online and will be able to see patients' reviews of their healing success. People will much more trust energy practitioners' clients' write-up's, NOT allopathic doctors that simply give Big Pharma poison pills to pop.

Let me step to the side and say this: start by opening in your mind a newly-painted doorway and explore putting holistic principles into a fourth, fifth or even higher dimensional framework in your life. Empower yourself with knowledge by searching the Internet under key words used in this chapter, this book, and other books of like progression. Remember that a new understanding in medicine and healing can take you to a whole new level in multi-dimensional living good health. Even though you may be saying that you cannot see, nor touch, smell, feel or taste these energetic connecting lines in your daily life of a three-dimensional reality or experience, it IS accessible to us in higher forms of consciousness that everyone ... repeat, all of us, can access.

You first have to be willing to accept there is so much more than just the space in front of you and around you. There is so much more. You CAN experience beyond what your senses normally show and tell you. We all have the key to release this padlock, but first it is important to distance yourself by radically decreasing a brainwashing that most don't even know occurs: watching television. Sitting in front of the plasma screen causes your mind to be brainwashed by the overwhelmingly violent or negative programming. In this book, I cite many other things you can do so that your true Self can become 'unchained' from the control centers from Big Brother government, Big Pharma, toxins in the food and water, chemtrails and so much more. In addition, give yourself breaks from technology: so many people are now either 'trapped' in front of a monitor, or addicted to a computer screen or other mobile device. They cannot put it down; they cannot get up; and they cannot stop checking for electronic mail. In fact, they suffer withdrawal symptoms, and have personality changes if they are away from their technology. The problem becomes one in which soon a whole generation is quickly becoming out of tune with not only nature but their natural intuitive abilities too.

Open The Flow Of Your Prosperity

Once we realize internally and acknowledge many new levels of perception, wakefulness and knowledge that is not taught in mainstream, and is in fact secluded from us by governments, powerful organizations and other control streams, we can then attain incredible new heights of joy in our lives.

Once you understand and believe in going higher (in an energetic state) and increasing the sensitivity level of your observation in life, you open the 'flow' of your prosperity thereby dramatically increasing your abundance including tapping into Source to realize some of the best health benefits in your life.

Some may be thinking I am talking in riddles, but when you just understand and want to grasp onto a new vine of wisdom, away from the power center on top of you, then an awakening occurs.

An awakening occurs especially when your energetic health is optimal. I am talking about the vibrational nature of your entity that shifts your health to better or worse. That vibration is affected by your thoughts, your actions, your emotions, your knowledge, your beliefs, and so much more. This incredible power works the other way too: the vibration in your environment (where you live, where you work, the air you breathe, etc.) has an immense effect upon your body, mind and immunity.

THE HUMAN POPULATION WILL SEE WITH UNCLOUDED EYES

This shift will happen so that the human population will see with unclouded eyes. It is Divine intervention. This is the incredibly important key of what is happening at this time.

> The coming vibrational shift, catalyzed by magnetic changes in the sun and expanding star systems next to ours pummeling in an array of different energies into our galactic field, will rid the veil that is constantly drawn across our awakening consciousness by those who try to govern us in negative and inhumane ways.

As Gaia, Mother Earth, receives this new energy, it will change our consciousness, including affecting our bodies, our minds, our emotions and our electromagnetic fields. As we soak up more of this new Light, the vibration of our be-ing will be transformed, and as a population, we will overcome the darkness.

Of course, the key to this shift is getting more rest, more sleep and more time to connect to Source (Divine, One, and Higher Self). We are all being bathed, and from this rinsing, there is chaos as the Establishment sees more are gaining older wisdoms. Older energies that have kept us away from knowing how to heal through natural energies are trying their hardest to keep us in the dark.

Forces such as the Military Industrial Complex are keeping us in fear by starting new wars and conflicts. Governments are keeping us from knowing more about other celestial beings, from the most wondrous energies to power-up industry, and from other dimension knowledge like portals that they use themselves. Instead, the Establishment is keeping us in the "modern Stone Age". But these darker forces cannot win the end game.

> As we shift our sleep patterns -- the golden key to transformation -- to become the central axis of our lives, away from a controlled way of life -- and this new consciousness becomes painfully yet astonishingly apparent -- we each will then renovate our Self and the passion and goal of life will be to create and swim in joy and simplicity, not get bogged-down with debt and material-based ego and tethered in a slave-like manner to technology.

Are you feeling the cosmic change? Are you experiencing a vibrational shift in your own life? If yes, join the Skyaia® community online and share your experience with those that can appreciate your journey and provide you with other advice. Many unique energies are coalescing. As you go through this alteration, I will say that you will feel very tired at times, and you could even sometimes feel like the biggest bipolar candidate in the world. Your relationships with people, even family members, will change; you may even sever ties with some individuals you have known for many years. No, you're likely not going crazy; you are just ridding those older energies that are keeping you on your belly when all you want to do is fly.

PRIORITIZING SLEEP OVER EVERYTHING ELSE: GOOD SLEEP BEFORE GOOD LIFE

Remember the key -- and I have to say it yet again: sleep more. It is the most important way to reduce any potentially deleterious effects in your life. Many individuals will say that they don't have time to sleep more. One must prioritize. Make no mistake about it -- so many of those that choose to continue running faster and faster on the hamster treadmill of life will break-down mentally

first, then emotionally, then electromagnetically then physically. Those that put their health first will 'pass through' this big vibrational shift effectively.

In chapters ahead, I will talk about the darker forces that want you to stay trapped below the veil and not experience the transformation. There will be a lot that don't 'pass through' this vibrational shift, and as a result, they will become mentally ill and/or become under governmental control. Of course, this all seems a figment of the imagination and probably delusional to quite a few, but I am talking to the masses that are willing to hear a different voice of reasoning, to look at the very big picture of life beyond what most know on a daily level, and to those that want to experience a new way of life better understanding the multi-dimensional reality that we can access and thereby live more joyously.

You can change the paradigm. You can be a part of it. Start now.

CHAPTER 5

OUR DESTINY DEPENDS ON YOUR MIND

How Mind Energy Can Create Abundance Or Lack In Your Life

As His High Holiness the Dalai Lama has said, "It is very important to contemplate the true nature of the inner mind."

I will be blunt and say it outright: the "secret" in life to maximizing abundance (not just money, but love, joy health, peace, protection, and all that good stuff) is to think positive and create a shielding energy barrier around yourself, your family, your home, your business, and whatever else you want to shelter from negative entities and harmful energy streams. Think positive by very carefully watching your thoughts and your attitude. Guard your body and mind and everything else you want to defend by commanding the Universe. Say it out loud and forcibly, but it must be a conscious shift that you make happen by making sure two things happen: first, that you really and truly believe you are actually changing your destiny in a positive way and do not have any doubts that it will not work; and, second, you say it with love (never doubt or fear or anger) in your voice. That is, think joyful things when you say it. Don't be meek. Remember how your parents told you, 'Speak up!'? Well, get out there and say it out loud in your car while driving down the highway listening to Pink Floyd's "Shine On Your Crazy Diamond", in the shower or bathtub, in the garden while planting new bulbs or raking leaves, upon getting up to start a new day of infinite possibilities, and so forth.

Everyone has the right to think and judge, although this is perhaps lesson one in mind energy – if you wish to bring abundance into your life, one must be open to learning new things. We judge those different to us when we know little about the subject of judgment. I realize you can easily look-up the definition of an altered state but permit me to explain it in terms of doing something good for yourself rather than feeling odd or afraid to tell someone else you too have them. The truth is millions of people have altered states because our creator gave us the ability to harness incredible amounts of energy with our minds.

Some will believe that altered states can only be brought on by street drugs or pharmaceutical components. And it is true that altered states can occur by those methods. Even though I have never ever tried either of those means, I can tell you those paths are negative and the degree of abundance or lack in your life – which is what this chapter is all about – is certainly tipped to the side of deficiency or poverty.

As vibrations in the natural states of our planet continue to shift, there will soon be a time when altered states are something that will be readily accepted. Someone might ask, "What did you do yesterday?" and the reply might be, "Oh, nothing much, I had a great altered state and was able to better understand my next stepping stone in life". I am not embarrassed to tell you that I regularly have altered states. I have awe-inspiring meditational sessions that are panoramic in multi-dimensions. This is how I can tap into a clairvoyant, clairsentient, and clairaudient gift. These experiences create so much abundance for me. They give me direction because I am more connected to my Higher Self. Why should I even be self-conscious of these wonderful experiences? If you are having naturally-induced altered states, share them with others, write about them, be proud of them and teach / show others how to have them. Again, like I always say, empower yourself to learn something new. There are wondrous other books out there, and perhaps the Skyaia® website will one day soon have a list of them, especially from authors that have written in to advise how their book / information can help someone grow in new evolutionary ways.

TRANSCENDENCE IS MIND-BASED

We already know that different emotions affect our cells, even our DNA and even more -- our spiritual journey and connection to One / Source / God. Just check out guru Greg Braden's research to know more. Your emotions can not only affect your internal structure, ability to attract positive or negative events, and even alter your longevity, but also your sentiments, feelings, sensations and other thoughts -- essentially your mind-set -- can impact someone else's internal composition.

Let me say this very directly: you can even cause an infection or disease in someone else just by the way you think around them, talk to them, or touch them. Unless it is direct or indirect self-defense, only negative people will harm others, so watch what you think. Your thought stream is very powerful. On the other positive side of the coin, you can also help someone overcome grief, defeat an illness, or lift them up to new heights in life just from the way your energetic stream of consciousness enters that other person's personal space. We can all transcend. Like anything positive that brings rewards, it takes practice (a more positive word than work).

THE MEANING OF LIFE IS DIRECTLY PROPORTIONAL TO THE ENERGY OF YOUR MIND

Life is rising above negative actions: gossip, the 'he said she said' hearsay, the odious acts that one neighbor may do upon another neighbor, revenge against another's lower evolution, jealousy, anger, and so forth.

Life is not about competitively outdoing someone else, for not only is there no joy by thinking or being told you are worse than someone else, but also there is no joy beyond the present moment by thinking or being told you are better than someone else. Life is akin to yoga: concentrate on your own growth. If the person in a yoga class can put her / his feet behind their neck, and you cannot, the second you feel defeated and say "I can't do that" is the moment you have mentally sent your cells a negative vibrational message that can energetically change your entire path forward.

Life is about excelling in the output of love -- both for yourself and others (both those you know and so-called strangers, even though technically in energetic terms nobody is a stranger since we are all part of One or Source). Divine Intelligence of the Universe operates through love. And since each of us is connected to the umbilical cord of the Universe, the birthplace of our origins, increasing Abundance in life is all about be-ing in love with your path and acting in love for yourself and others. These sentences likely do not enter our subconscious on first read, so it is a good idea to re-read the few paragraphs above so these concepts sink in. The goal each day is to mentally go beyond worrying about the future (which is living deficiently) and just be in the present moment where the mathematical and Divine Universe is sentiently pulsating.

The meaning of life is different. That is why I say the meaning of life is directly proportional to your mind. To those that think in negative terms, the meaning of life is, 'life is a bitch then you die'. To those that think in positive terms, even those that overcome truly enormous challenges and defeats, the meaning of life is a path of wonderful experiences where one can maximize joy to Self and others, help others along their paths without giving so much of Self to become needy, and to maximize one's gifts to move the planet forward in some way.

When the focus is on your own steps, and you never mentally compare your journey to someone else's, that is when the true path of abundance begins for you.

Once you commence each moment with joy and love, an energy field begins and then radiates outward. Sure, there are many moments where you may have to begin over to reset the joy and love so that the flow is continuous. Some have to begin every few seconds, and some that have practiced often may only have to start every day. As that field becomes bigger, so too does the magnetic ability to attract more abundance increase. To be, as a verb, is just to move your thoughts to positive things, and command the Universe to place your spiritual experience as a human being in the highest Flow. In short, life is all about transcendence. And similar to previous mentions that our minds are integral to evolutionary advances, transcendence is initiated by the mind. The next step, once this launch occurs, the goal is to connect to Universal Mind or One, which is the divine energy of That which Is.

Large Cycles & Dimensional Bending / Stacking

All while living, trying to figure out our 'place' and our 'purpose', one of the harder concepts for most of us is that time is not 'horizontal'. Even though we have words like yesterday, today and tomorrow, all these three so-called different periods (that we perceive as different) are all happening at the same time in multi-dimensional space. The particle flow of the Universe (what we call time) is 'stacked' vertically, so that literally, in an alternate dimension, upon accessing it, you can 'see' the dinosaurs, the Middle Ages, the year 2347. They are all happening now, yes, right now. You may say at this point, "Okay, Simon, that is where you lost me." But again, at any point, whenever I say something that seems unbelievable or incredible, research it and see what road it takes you down. I am certainly not here to waste your time or write a fairytale.

Sure, we cannot see dinosaurs in our three-dimensional space at this present moment in consciousness. I bet you are glad we can all agree on that! The reason we cannot is because throughout changes in the cosmos there have been many dimensional shifts or warps that have caused an entirely new energetic field to begin (and a resulting period of physical chaos has likely ensued). Evolution happens through inter-dimensional transference: when a new dimension arrives, the old (so to speak) goes out and the new comes in. The Mayans understood these larger periods. The Mayan Calendar began with the Fifth Great Cycle in 3114 BC and their calendar came to a close on December 21, 2012 AD. Obviously we know now that this was not the end of so-called time. It was the beginning of a new big cycle – a new dimensional field entry – which makes it very important and is very likely a big part of why this is so much of an Awakening going on as well as chaos going on at this time. Look up 'yuga' in translated Hindu scriptures. The Hindu Kali Yuga calendar began on February 18, 3102 B.C. and amazingly there is only a difference of 12 years between theirs and the Mayan Calendar. So both calendars began over 5,000 years ago, have very similar dates of when new cycles begin, and yet these two ancient cultures did not have any contact. If this has piqued your curiosity, and you are further interested in this 'big picture' of how time (outside of the cycles of life -- like lunar phases, sunrise/sunset, seasons, etc.) is really just a concept put upon us to govern and enslave society (i.e., make your paycheck proportional to the time you expend rather than be paid for your performance or value), there are some great books out there to get your hands on.

The Mayans may or may not have understood dimensional field 'bending' but they certainly understood large cycles, and yet ironically, even though they were so advanced in explaining these different epochs, they couldn't 'see' their own demise through larger-scale climate shifts (because the Mayan culture essentially came to an end due to a persistent and very intense drought).

When larger magnetic shifts occur not only on Earth but also in the cosmos, there are larger climate shifts on our planet. I will talk about this more in the chapters on climate.

When a larger magnetic shift or a shift in one or more energy fields occurs, it 'restacks' the dimensional 'output' of space. In other words, dimensions can shift, and one can become more dominant than the other, thereby allowing a certain species in one dimension to survive and another species in another dimension to be terminated, depending on the physical chaos that may or may not happen accompanying those shifts.

Of course this subject matter of dimensional shifts is very esoteric and complex. In mainstream, very little science or medicine, if any at all, is incorporated in this. For example, energy medicine now proves that when we can balance and fortify one's energy / electromagnetic field, one's health can be notably enhanced and so much dis-ease can be rid much more simply. Just look up Zeev Kolman and the field of bioenergetics to see how this transference of electromagnetic energy activates an intrinsically-intelligent natural healing process in a patient with any type of malady. Bioenergetic healing is aimed at correcting the aura. Since electromagnetic energy runs in meridian channels throughout our planet, bioenergetic healing can take place at a distance because at higher levels of consciousness, the healer can connect like points of energy and send them into a pinpointed location (very similar to programming GPS coordinates but through much higher refinement). Of course, too many allopaths attached to negative pathways don't want to even open their minds to this, but if you follow more peer-to-peer reviews (and not necessarily the peer-reviewed studies which so often are politicized or even controlled groups not letting in anything new that may threaten the so-called controlling status quo) you will see the incredible results being made for hundreds of thousands of people.

You can bet that the Establishment knows all about dimensional shifts: there is plenty of evidence in the direction of projects by DARPA and other militarized outfits that one of their major goals is to better understand portals, remote viewing, invisibility in warfare, and the power of electromagnetics to make weapons that kill people and computer / electrical systems but leave buildings intact.

In the future, I will likely write much more on the topic of "militarized electromagnetics", by connecting the dots and showing how the Establishment can control any human population just by changing the energetic vibration of a space because mentally we are all connected to a certain wavelength of energy. That is, the Earth pulsates vibrationally at a certain level, as proven by the Schumann Resonances (again, please look it up if you're not familiar with this concept because already this book covers so many topics), and since there is technology that can change the 'sequencing' of this Resonance, it thereby affects our mental wavelengths which can then cause us to react / act differently. There are certain frequencies to calm, and others to incite ... so think how powerful this is ... the Establishment could literally prevent a riot, or put a population in a 'slumber'.

Our destiny depends on your mind. Note that as our technological evolution progresses (not necessarily 'advances' per se), we are becoming more reliant on each other. We are a global village, as you have often heard. But it is much more than that: just look at the Fukushima radiation disaster to see how a 'world away' there are impacts, increasing every week, too close to home. This might be a bit esoteric but we all are separate ingredients that go into making a cake.

As technology gets more complex, and the Establishment uses more of their weapons against the People, it is increasingly important that we realize the true potential of our combined mind power before it is too late. If too many of us 'give up' due to fear of authority to the Establishment that is trying to take control of our minds, then our destiny will likely be much dimmer because our thoughts will be shackled by cerebral electromagnetic bracelets, and only the elite will be free from mind control.

Mind Control Technologies: The Race Is On

Mind control technologies exist in abundance already, but the next goal of the Establishment is to control your mind. The military, through DARPA and other dark-matter cabal units, know that planetary control can only be attained through control of the mind. Mind control technologies will become prolific if we do not counter the energy by collective mind power. And so the race is on.

Control is a word you will hear more and more in all forms and guises. It was the illusionist, Henry Kissinger, said that, 'he who controls energy controls the world'. You can't have an economy, even under a totalitarian regime, without energy. We often think of energy like that needed to mine minerals, transform resources, manufacture products, ship and deliver products, and so much more. But this was not necessarily the energy that Kissinger was talking about. He was talking about the energy he knows – the electromagnetic energy (including Tesla) that surpasses all nuclear and fossil fuel energy by a long shot. Even though the Establishment will see challenges from its enemies, like the advanced development of crypto-currency (aka Bitcoins is just the beginning) in the fear of major currencies going south, the endgame is won by those that manage and control the electromagnetic energy realm in the lower-physical dimensional world we live in. Then they can force everybody to do what the heck they want. Fortunately, this may never happen, but it's a goal in the eyes of the Establishment. We better believe it that Humanity is in the crosshairs of the Establishment's bow.

Before we go much further and deeper into this huge tunnel of 'Control or Freedom?', one main goal of this book is to ask you to empower yourself with (new) intelligence. Education is a lifelong process, and now, whether you are 17 or 71, is just as an important phase of your life to not only learn a part of the real story (of life) but also to share what you know with others. In the near future, there will be a huge body of alternative intel, and its goal will be to beat the Establishment at its own game. Type 'mind control technologies' into any search engine that is not part of the stroke-tracking Establishment (i.e., Google follows you).

As Pink Floyd sang, 'Welcome to the Machine', there is an overwhelming amount of evidence that confirms the existence of mind control projects, including those designed and proliferated by the CIA. Type in "MK-ULTRA" to a private search engine and see the extraordinary power that the Establishment gained starting back in the 1950s. MK-ULTRA, run by the CIA's Office of Scientific Intelligence, was a clandestine and criminal human experimentation program with the central pursuits wrapped around mind control. And it of course still exists today, just under a different name, even though the CIA and others will greatly deny it. It does not take much imagination to know how much technology has changed in sixty years, and what the new powers are in manipulating the realities of the masses (not just individuals one at a time). That's right: the manipulation is more efficient (in an evil way) now – in that more people can be 'commanded' in thought patterns not only against their will but also against their knowing they are being led to the guillotine.

GLOBAL EMANCIPATION CITIZENS UNITED

Make no mistake that mind control technologies are weapons that attack the 'last frontier' – to enslave the cerebral (mental) realm, to bring a force-field around one's brain that takes control, as in making someone into a obeying robot-like figurine. In the "old days", the Establishment used drugs, then they 'moved-up' to electromagnetic (EM) / microwave vibrational waves to destabilize a person's control over their own behavior, decisions and emotions. As earlier mentioned, these EM energies literally attack and take control of the brain and central nervous system. Then, as the CIA and others had 'fun' (the sick, arrogant sons of hell) in gaining increasing control, they have begun to use nanotechnologies (similar to experimentation used to alter climate now by putting nano-size particles that reflect sunlight to cause cooling because the Establishment thinks that the planet is warming up too fast, which is complete and utter nonsense to put it politely). Of course, now even in the news are electronic microchip implants embedded under the skin -- and of course there are "willing" participants -- there always are -- especially many more if those doing the experimentation provide some low pay for 'monitoring' the subject, or those doing the tormenting offer other forms of promise (aka as simple as food to those on welfare / food stamps, to 'cushy' jobs in FEMA Corps). Of course, the overwhelming majority have no idea that these 'sewn-in' chips create new nerve connections in different parts of the brain that alter their lives radically, and have power over thought, movement, emotions, and, drastically alter relationships, job performance, and overall living 'instructions'.

Look up the Air Force Research Laboratory and their patent on "neuro-electromagnetic" devices and see how they tie-in "pulse-modulated" microwave radiation to literally attach subliminal messages. Go down a deep rabbit hole by reading up on Voice to Skull technologies. Some think I am a conspiracy theorist, but they are either in denial or just don't want to discover what they fear could be true. Those that call me a conspiracy theorist are the 'perfect candidate' for the Establishment because they obey and follow orders and talk down those human 'brothers and sisters' like myself that are trying to get through their thick skulls to talk some sense into them. So much of Mainstream Media of course then follow through with commands by the Establishment to make people like myself look like conspiracy

theorists (although I give my full support in crediting many radio stations and some TV stations like RT.com, which bend-away from the Establishment to reach out to the growing numbers that know more and want more so-called 'alternative knowledge'). Fortunately, due to the shifting energies on the planet at this important time, a large number are literally 'waking-up', are taking a leap of faith, and are realizing how they are controlled. It is a huge process for any individual but it must be done. We all must realize that freedom is the ultimate need in the meaning of life. Once this realization of freedom happens, the mind is on a completely different circuit. Imagine thousands then millions of me's and you's, writing and communicating and spreading this type of information, in justifying the emancipation of our freedom as sovereign citizens of Earth. It's what I call: Global Emancipation Citizens United -- freedom for all, all people united we stand.

THE BIGGEST RACE IS ON

The biggest race is on: will Humanity lose their freedom in the 'new' electromagnetic "neuro shackles" that the Establishment is increasingly putting on us (through the air, through our drinking water, through our food, through our telecommunication devices, in penetration of our own auras, and so much more)? Or, will civilization, outside of the shape-shifting reptilian Illuminati and their slaves, wake-up in time, use its combined mind power and re-write the "future" so that the Establishment cannot take hold of our intrinsic desire to be free?!?

To review, the development of mind control methods and technologies goes back decades to even before the 1950s. Concentration camp inmates were 'used' by the Nazi tyranny in too many grotesque ways, again starting with mind controlling drugs. Nowadays, researchers have shown that they can read someone's mind by remotely -- yes, distantly -- measuring their cerebral activity! Individuals can even have information and memories "extracted" without them even knowing -- until of course they remember that they cannot recollect certain events or bits of data they once recorded.

Just be warned: satellites, television (through mnemonic circles and advanced technologies), mobile transmission masts (including emitting frequencies 'hidden' on cell towers) and more are ways mind control technologies can take control. I do not have any television in my household, and for good reason. Obviously, do not be paranoid, but it is being proved that it is good to be in control of your life, and reduce the ways that the Establishment can get at (and "into") you. Oh, I know, it all sounds crazy, but the information here is a number of wavelengths ahead, so as to protect you and give you warning(s) so you can prepare in time.

I will re-visit this subject later in the book. For now, I will say with strong condemnation that the government's atrocities of torture, abuses and weapons upon the 'last frontier' of the mind is not only extremely unlawful but despicable.

OUR DESTINY DEPENDS ON YOUR MIND & MY MIND

Let me end this chapter by saying that our destiny depends on how you think, how I think and how everyone thinks. We can create our own future in the Now (in this present moment). What we think together, in group consciousness, provides us lack or abundance going forward.

> For this reason, it is so important that you do not 'feed into' the brainwashing of the Establishment. The goal of the Establishment is to put you and I into fear mode. They start wars, many times purposefully through constant aggression. They want us cowering, they don't want you or I doing any critical thinking like the concepts and discussion in this book.

The final chapter of this book talks about the largest threat that will likely face us all as a planet. Fortunately, we have a choice and we have the ability to get through it. There is just one 'but'. Isn't there always? The 'but' is ... "But the Establishment wants to be in control and not allow us to know much about what is likely coming / going to happen." The Establishment wants to keep you and me in the dark. I think I can say that if you're reading this book, then you're with me on this one – and I am ... we together ... are not going to allow this to happen.

The Establishment tells you that their technology will be able to save you from upcoming celestial challenges, but their promises are nothing but disguised weaponry. The Establishment cannot be trusted, and it is my prediction that history will show they will lose the race that I talked about earlier. Their evil transgressions and their disobedience in following the humanitarian principles of love and peace will not gain over us when we THINK over / above them.

Only through energetic fields filled with love, and a mass consciousness awakening joined at the cerebral / mental level which is connected to Source (the Divine Intelligence of the Universe), at a reliably steady and determined level of positivity, will allow us to move through this next wave of evolution.

CHAPTER 6

REALIZING OUR BIRTH-GIVEN RIGHT TO FREEDOM

Reprogramming Your Life The Way You Want It To Be

There is profound wisdom in the interconnectedness of science and spirituality. Everything has a vibration. When you are ill, you have a different vibration humming from your body and mind compared to when you are well. The tide has an incredible vibration: it is so in-tune with its surroundings. A tree when cut down gives off a different vibration to a healthy tree standing tall. A pregnant woman has a different vibration as two be-ings growing and learning to communicate and interact as one compared to a female child or adult by herself. A male has a different energetic vibration to a female (that's why I love John Gray's concept of "Men are from Mars, and Women are from Venus"). The vibrations or rocks shift as they are shaped by water and wind. The vibration of the earth under a community of homes is going to be different if the ground was once a graveyard compared to a once pristine field. Ley lines cause different energies to spread-out depending on their shape / formation: just look-up the crystalline structure of our planet's energy ley lines to understand alignments and 'sacred' geometry. You send-out a different vibration if you exert a few spurts of anger compared to when you are sleeping peacefully. The force-fields of these realms of energy pulsate outward until they are absorbed, modified, reflected, or destroyed.

Mother is the energetic word for God or Source or One. The stars come from the womb of universal creation. The earth we live on is our cosmically-generated mum. We live IN God. Mother Earth (Gaia) is alive and breathing: Mama exhales and inhales – and we connect energetically to that Gaia (planetary) breath. As the planet coughs, we are disturbed thereof. The Gaia hypothesis was formulated by James Lovelock and Lynn Margulis four decades ago, and was of course initially received with aggressive opposition by a lot in the scientific community, which some may say will be the action taken to some of my material in this book – but remember – I (just like you) have energetic programming power – and I now command that many are reading the discussion in this book, many are absorbing it positively and the concepts are helping people in multiple disciplines and journeys, And So It Is (note the necessary use of present tense verbs to command something in the universe).

The Principle Choice Is To Realize Your / Our Freedom

The objective of your daily life is to be cognizant of your vibration, and moreover, to optimize the energy you output. For most of us, our minds are tapered to a physical manifestation. You know, the 'what am I doing today?' kind of thinking. 'I have this to do and that to get', or 'I wish I didn't have that problem on my hands right now'.

The choice we have is to realize our freedom. We can allow our minds to reach new depths of the universe. I'm talking going beyond the current three-dimensional space of thought, the daily living sphere that so many of us get trapped into. Now you may say, "Simon, that's all very well and nice, but HOW do I do it, how do I get there? I really DO want to increase my be-ing into a greater number of dimensions where the so-called gurus sitting upon mountain tops can apparently so easily slip into."

To repeat from earlier, the first step is to command it so … and then the second step is to BELIEVE it so, that what you want to happen will actually happen. But these two steps can be very challenging for so many, mainly because so many of us have never really learned HOW to believe. Most of all, with some exceptions like the totally deranged or some of the psychotic lunatics that run countries, can exit the 'trap' of regular consciousness and actually connect with the Divine, what I refer to as the 'source-code' of the program that we call life. Funny that, most would say life is a game, and of course, in a certain perspective it is a diversion, whether joy or competition, but that game, no matter how you look at is, is a program. Life could be a game or a program that is for entertainment / pleasure or competition / dispute. Life can be made as an active pursuit of leisure, not struggle, war or rivalry. The Establishment trains and programs us that life is a struggle but the reality is it is the opposite. Once you break free from these chains, you discover the other side. Perhaps this is what some famous music bands sing about. Since there is a big difference between a programmed game and a programmable game, this essentially means you can make the music of life, and not be one of the players who is programmed. Re-read this paragraph if you feel frustrated in not grasping it. I never said it's easy, but it is most attainable with patience, sending out a positive energy 'broadcast signal', ... and BELIEVING you can do it.

If you want to hit the jackpot and tap on the door to God, you have to be the one to program it to happen, because if you are out there waiting for the program to take you to God, it just "ain't" gonna happen. Through all the programming laid upon us, we wait and wait and wait far too much: that is why we, as a country, as a society, cannot break from the antagonism, we cannot stop the mentality that we have an opposition. Instead, simply stop the competition, be the yoga master, and then your energetic force-field shifts both inside you and around you. It is so powerful that it changes your friends, your activities and then what you receive.

Re-Program Life The Way You Want It To Be

Go back to the chapter title: this is all about connecting to a Divine. I meet a lot of people, and some tell me that they cannot truly feel the connection to God (or a divine entity, celestial be-ing, or creative force in a spiritual but not religiously dutiful perspective). I ask them a few questions of what they are doing, and they tell me they pray or meditate or reflect -- all with the same goal in mind, just different ways to reach the One Spirit that connects us all. I nod my head and then I ask them about their attitude and their perseverance and their daily living style -- and that is where I am polite when I tell them that is where they break the connection. If you are seeing life as a non-stop array of problems, then your ability to connect to Source Code is increasingly limited depending on how programmed you are or have become. Forgive me for sounding like I'm giving a sermon, but you have limited power to connect to Divine when you are caught-up in praising the wrong things in your life.

If you are really down on life and complain a lot, and don't see much as beautiful, and you concentrate on problems that may come your way, the Universe is going to mirror more of that into your life. Life is a big mirror. The thoughts you give out are emulated or echoed right back at you. If you are in retail and you're constantly thinking, "I can't do this, I don't know if I'm going to get this sale," then there is a much higher probability you won't get the deal, compared with the person that says or thinks, "I'm going to do my best, and I believe and know that everything is in flow, and I command all positive forces to come together to bat for me so I get this ticket," then the vibration of that more affirmative and optimistic person is going to be felt at a level above the three-dimensional space, such that the

Universal energy will be unconsciously humming to bring about success. Remember that this positive energy field takes a consistent series of thoughts to increase the likelihood that some form of Abundance will show, and then once you have developed a certain strength of magnetic attractiveness you will see the Flow increase. This is the expression, 'when it rains it pours', because when we truly can concentrate on connecting with Divine Intelligence, we can then attract more Abundance into our lives.

It Is All About The Vibration: Connection To Energetics

That is the important word here: vibration. Know there is an energetic pulsation from every thought that comes from your mind. Let's talk about something I call a "Source-moment". This is, with all religion aside, a fleeting but ever-memorable flash of cerebral electricity that I personally know when you realize your connection to a higher force. When you have a Source-moment, you know that one of the most important, if not THE most important things in day-to-day living is to manage your thoughts so that you, not someone else or society, can live your life the way it is truly meant to be lived. All of a sudden, you are programming life the way you want it to be. You are no longer being programmed. Remember, programming (aka manifestation for YOU) is the moment of Now, the present; but programmed (aka indoctrination) is you living by someone else's rules and forever set in concrete in the past.

How To Truly Quit Smoking

One example of being programmed is the incredibly powerful control method of smoking. It goes way beyond the nicotine addiction that most doctors tell you. Some of the actual substances (over a thousand toxins) in a cigarette keep you 'controlled' energetically. That is right – a cigarette's power has the ability to enter and control your energetic layer – your highest health parameter (remember the five layers of health, the energetic layer being of the most important). Permit me to digress by saying that those of you that smoke are under a state of control. Your mind is controlled energetically. Most that smoke are aware of the increasingly tumultuous degradation of all those toxic chemical substances that smash and pound against the body, mind and spirit contained in first-hand, second-hand and even third-hand smoke derived from cigarettes (including the "new" electronic kind), and cigars. So why are there so many people that cannot stop smoking if they know the harm it is causing them? The research runs deep – and I will just say this for now: a surprisingly large percentage of the billions of dollars that come into the cigarette industry collectively is put into research; but this is not just simple research, this is incredibly complex investigation into the mind. Governments support – yes support – the cigarette companies (even though at times it appears that they lash out at them with millions of dollars in fines). It is all a game: governments under The Agenda want to know the same thing as the cigarette companies – how to control one's mind. Most smokers know it is simply not worth inviting an energy that carries with it the potential to cause dis-ease and most likely an earlier and many-a-time painful death. But here is that path that smokers have to go down to quit: simply put, any form of smoking changes your cellular vibration. If down deep – at the heart chakra level – you know the possibility of getting sick or you feel guilty for smoking in the first place – you are literally playing with fire – because you are attracting a similar negative type of energy in the Universe. Yes, at a subconscious level, you are asking the dis-ease to come into you. One gets addicted because some of the "advanced" chemicals in a cigarette turn-off one's self-esteem and distance one's conscious energy from optimal in programming the smoker that s/he doesn't truly love oneself. Nobody would knowingly wish to harm him/herself unless there is self-doubt, or lack of self-esteem (aka "I don't love myself as much as I could" type of thinking). If you have an overall feeling of despair in getting past the programmed energetics of life, reach for something where you feel inspired to go beyond your own self-annihilating limits, learn to love yourself and the planet, and see that every connective energy is there to teach us something. Quit today with amazing energetic medicine or kinesiology that has the power to reverse this negative programming and return you to a state of Skyaia® equilibrium: others are finding true energetic solutions, not just more toxic solutions like the 'patch' which can further make your health negative. Empower yourself to be greater, that of which your Higher Self is inviting you to become. For those smokers, go see a kinesiologist, energy healer, shamanic healer, or one with specialized knowledge in resetting your energetic balance. THAT is the key to quit successfully, once and for all.

Re-Program Your Journey

Break out of the mold, do it in the Now, shrug off those walls of powers that are separating your Self, and re-program your journey. I know some of you feel as if you are super-glued or you have been dropped down an iron-cast tube with re-bar cement all around you with hardly an inch to move. But I am telling you this: I may not even know you, but even before I connect to you, I know you CAN do it. How so? Because we are all connected energetically. I know you can break through, because the most powerful thing you can do for yourself is to feel the Flow of energetics working in your favor. The most influentially affirmative thing you can ever have in your life is knowing in your heart, knowing in the depth of your soul, that you have finally touched Divine Intelligence. That is when your life changes in a spark, and you sit down and say, 'Dang, what the heck was that electric spark I just hit?!' And it's going to feel something in between a chipmunk kiss and floating on a cloud.

Both are incredible, you'll just have to take my word for it if you haven't yet felt it (but will), and if you are currently saying 'Yuck!' to the thought of a chipmunk kiss, it is something so unique that there is literally no other way to describe it except to say that in a way the thought of it is so strange yet so beautiful, it causes laughter, mirth and delight just by thinking about it.

Our Origins Are Birthed From Beyond Earth

We come from the cosmos, from the stars, from remnants of light energy. Skyaia® says that everything is connected from our origins to the present moment. But remember one thing: that is thinking in time, our world on Earth. In the Universe, when we think of space, there is no time. There is be-ing, a state of now; and there is space movement (i.e., quasars, black holes, anti-matter collapse, etc.) There really wasn't a beginning, and there isn't an end either. There is not going to be an end. When you can see life this way, we worry not about death. Sure, those that live onward emotionally and vibrationally miss those that die, but I say I am not preoccupied with death because I know I never die. I move on ... I transform ... and the light that inside me, which is a part of God, a part of the Universe, transcends into the journey that I am on. Look at the universe as a 'loop'. People ask, 'well, what was there before the so-called 'Big Bang'? Well, first, the 'Big Bang' is all myth, just another parable or legend to have us believe in what the Authority Figure wants us to know. There has been many "big bangs": they are happening all the time. There are expansions, contractions; there is growth and there is decay.

Our origins are birthed from beyond this blue planet. The rays of light from above our sky, from a galaxy 100 million light years away, is connected to your cellular energy, no matter how micro-infinitesimally from perhaps billions of years ago (in reality, from other dimensions in non-time). Just like it must be so that someone living today is related through their DNA to that of Jesus', Buddha's, Mohammad's and other highly-evolved be-ings' genetic material. Each of us then chooses karmically to be birthed into the womb of our mother. Energetically, at a higher level of the many dimensions that exist, for this lifetime on planet Earth, we choose our mother, and depending on our karma (the energy of our journey) we decide the place we are born where that female is waiting to give birth to us so that your spirit has a 'shell', again in this lifetime. Sure, this may sound nuts, but when you philosophically and scientifically dissect so much of what has been taught to us, it doesn't fly in the wind.

Do Not Be Fooled: Alien Life Is Already Here

Some be-ings, not human, do not need a shell, and are just sheer light, plasma or even anti-matter. They have transcended beyond a casing and do not need a sheath any longer. On planet Earth, there are already other types of energy that are living, birthed from other galactic systems, and either come here haphazardly on meteorites or plasma, or actually are so advanced they 'transport' instantaneously here through dimensional shifts and vibrational morphing to survive such a 'journey' (remember there is no time so they are "re-stacking" the dimensional field). These be-ings do not likely or necessarily have a "head" and two arms, two legs and a mouth. That concept is only going horizontally with little progress in conceptuality because we are looking into the reflection of our own humanity. So-called aliens, which I think are better known as celestial be-ings, do not come to earth in so-called spaceships. This is all a play on your imagination which has been progressively programmed by the Establishment. Sure, I do not doubt the ancient pictographs showing 'visitors' in bubbles in the sky. They were likely light energy orbs, or they were mind-seeded projected visions projected intra-realities and/or 'birthed' through interwoven dimensional shifts. Okay, look … yes, this is all bizarre language. It IS complex, and there is SO much out there. You, me, us all – we have been dumbed-down, and you and I received the 'simple account, the "version 1.0", so we didn't have to question much. You have been 'played'; you have been spoken down to … since birth … unless these new concepts were taught to you. Shoot, I'm not the only one that is speaking like this, although perhaps I will say it is rare for someone like myself to be this direct about so many important issues as I am describing.

Will I be the first scientist to come out on television to say, "Absolutely, with 100% certainty, there are cosmic entities, other than humans, on Planet Earth"? In some ways, yes. But there will be copycats … yet beyond a certain point, there is going to be incredible momentum with this topic of "aliens". Everybody on the planet wants to know – and at SOME point, the Establishment will make a crisis (go to no waste) and they will create a 'False Flag' in some psychopathic way to show that aliens exist – but the Establishment will be the one fooling too many that it will be the Daddy figure rescuing humanity from the aliens.

All this is so hard to explain because we really do not have even the language to describe such advancements of concepts that originate from space. And do not forget, when we talk about this type of other journey, it does not relate to time, it relates to dimensionally-bending (/-bent) distance. Advanced be-ings are not going to go 500 thousand light years and wait 4 months or 20 years to get here, no matter how "fast" their transportation may be (and yes, there really is 'faster' than the speed of light; there is even initial proof of this in the scientific community). All this 'speed of light' talk is a bunch of codswallop.

Celestial be-ings do not have so-called "spaceships" that are joined by screws the size of our arms, or even magnetically-sticking hulls. Any transport vessel that has to go through space worms is not going to exist – because there are too many forces that will 'vanish' it (aka break it up or 'swallow' it without a trace). This is the first thing we have to get out of our minds. Advanced be-ings are going to be able to manipulate extra-dimensional space, they are going to be able to curve, slow-down, accelerate, and combine light with other forces that are not even known to us. We have to comprehend that cosmic entities – other than those non-intelligent microbes getting here on meteorites) – use energies that do not use time as a concept. Their transportation is their energy source.

For human be-ings, our truest and most powerful transportation source of the highest kind is from and through our mind and our heart. Yes, we travel through our mind and our heart, into other dimensions, and this is the real key to setting new intentions for our planet.

Because of advancements that are literally light years beyond ours (or beyond the dimensions we function in), most of these celestial beings have to be peaceful. Sure, there are dark forces out there, and there is a lot of research that hypothesizes and even shows negative cosmic entities. And I truly believe that Earth has both Light Cosmic Be-ings and Dark Cosmic Be-Ings, and our planet is literally in the 'throes' of these forces. We may not agree there, but let me say something you will agree with: through the Establishment's increasingly relentless bombardment of crap in our lives, it is the overwhelming minority of humans that exude the war-mongering, hateful, vengeful, ego-maniacal ideas that cause the decay in too much for so many. THIS is what we MUST reverse – and I believe we CAN do it when we join together, as we are indeed doing in our current Awakening. I am so very, very tired of The War Machine that we keep pretending must exist in order to get us more 'advanced'. It is all backwards! We must walk away from physically harming others and use our cerebral powers to attain peace: THAT is the Greyhound bus I am on in journeying across the Land in my Dream of reality.

As I progress into different volumes of Skyaia®, I will talk much more about alien energies and what is likely on the horizon, especially in Volume 2: but what is essential to know right now is that it is crucial for human civilization to move beyond the programming of the Establishment and to realize that Source Code is mathematically benevolent. Are you digging me on that one? The universe is arithmetically benign, generous and giving. And if you can't agree with me on that, perhaps your world has been taught to you as one in which you have to fight your way through it:? Then no wonder you cannot agree with me. You can hit the 'start over' button to re-program, move onto the train track that is not filled with the spooks in the dark, and get on with making your splash in the world to make That Which Is a better place for you and others.

Once we, as a race, are able to poke through the web of lies that are spun all around us, and see that celestial be-ings from very negative to very positive energy fields are here on Planet Earth (and have been for millions of years), then we will begin to move forward in many great ways, instead of living in a faked or even "counterfeited" reality full of fear and control.

We must break-out and attain our true freedom – by living IN the heart, expanding our energy of love to all, and journeying cerebrally as a part of the Mind of the Universe.

THIS IS WHERE WE ACCELERATE TO JOIN TOGETHER IN PURPOSE

Parts of this, or much of this may still be fuzzy at this point. Often when we need to clear an old pond, upon stepping-in we cloud-up the water. It takes time to allow the heavy silt to settle, and so in being a little more than a third through the book, turn-up your senses because this is where we really start to accelerate to join together in purpose.

CHAPTER 7

PLUG IN TO DIVINE, YOUR CONNECTION TO ENERGETIC SOURCE

Empower Self By Listening To Cosmic Guidance

There once was a very old and very wise frog called Great Granddad. Every morning, after having breakfast with all the other mama, papa and children frogs, he would jump off to some place that nobody knew where he went. One day, in expecting his return home at the exact same time every day, the children frogs had all gathered around the lily table a little earlier than usual awaiting their dinner. They all wanted to know where Great Granddad went every day, for they had given up looking for him on countless occasions.

But one exceptionally smart little girl frog said, "Great Granddad, why do you hide from us every day? We can never find you, and we want to know where you go?"

Old Great Granddad could see the earnestness in her eyes, and said, "First, I do not and will never hide from you. But I cannot tell you where I go. Second, if you ever have a question for me in the future, do not wait so long until you ask me. I may not be able to tell you the exact answer, but it is always best never to hold anything inside you."

A little boy frog then jumped-up and said, "We won't tell anyone if you tell us, we promise! Please, please, please tell us where you go every day."

Great Granddad replied: "If you tell someone else about where I go, it could put me in danger. I might get eaten by a snake or an eagle. I can only tell you when you get to my age. Then I will reveal my secret."

But then the tiniest frog in the back who had just learned to rivet-speak said in an unusually loud voice for her age and size, "But Great Granddad, how do you expect us to survive until your old age if we don't have anywhere to hide? What if the snake or the eagle finds us and eats us up because we don't have a very good hiding place like yours?

Old Great Granddad was shocked at her intellect and wisdom for such a young age. Everyone was very quiet because they were just deciphering what this little young frog had just said.

"Okay then," sighed Old Great Granddad. "I will tell you, because you are more wise than me. I realize now I was selfish not to tell you, because I was only thinking about my own safety, my own protection and my own life. I regret I did not think about you all as much as I should have done. You are right. You need to have the best protection possible. Just do me a favor, and listen very carefully here: you must pass on this secret to all other frogs and tell them to always act with altruism. But remember to tell them to honor the code of silence so that you don't cross the line and become a danger for everyone you love and care about. I made a mistake and acted by being too silent. It is a very fine line: if you are too silent, you become selfish and then jeopardize the safety and lives of those around you; if you are too noisy, you become conceited and you too jeopardize the safety and lives of those around you. You must always try to use your best judgment in balancing the needs for the greatest good."

The children frogs were a bit stunned. Great Granddad had given one of his long sermons, and some of it had gone over the children frog's heads. Nevertheless, he proceeded to tell the children of his hiding place secret.

"I find the biggest lotus flower pad, and I crawl in between the big cushy leaves and I make sure I am really well hidden so that the snake and the owl cannot see me. It's a perfect hiding spot."

"Ahhh, wow!" said the children froggies in unison.

"Today…" started Great Granddad, "…you have taught me a very valuable lesson. You have shown me that even though I may have lived to have the longest frog life ever, I will never stop learning. I must always be open to learning new lessons along the way, no matter where they come from, and no matter who may tell or show me. I must share the important lessons I learn, for the advice and gift I shall receive back shall be more than twice as important for not only me but for the collective good."

All the children frog and Great Granddad slurped up their special slug-n-fly dinner in silence. They had a lot to think about.

The next day, the frogs all found really cool hiding places under many different lotus flowers, and for the first time in their lives, they felt that much safer. But the bigger realization was they also felt all the more connected to not only Great Granddad for his trust and protection but perhaps moreso to the greater energy that allowed them to increase their wisdom together.

And of course, all froggies lived happily ever after.

Looking At Life In An Energetic Way, Beyond Three-Dimensions

We must all look way "outside of the box" and go well beyond our current definition of perception. We must look inter-dimensionally and multi-dimensionally to understand and grab a hold onto advancing our science and our spirituality. For in this threading of discipline and mysticism lies the true ability of our future. We cannot continue for more than ten generations without first just merely acknowledging that we, and the trees, and insects and birds and all creatures have vibrations that feel pain and have knowledge of love. Once the souls of our children, streaming in from other galaxies at this time (the reason we call them "Star Children") reach forward beyond our current "normal" three-dimensional reality on Earth and see things that are so fantastically beautiful and serene, centered around non-violence and respect for all living energies, then and only then can we start to re-mold the way we interact and harness the strengths we need to gather in order to guarantee that our children's grandchildren's grandchildren survive. This is why I say that two of the most important things you can do in growing spiritually on a daily level is to love as much as possible, and love all matter knowing that everything holds a vibration – and – to know that you are capable of mind and heart travel, and in that realization, you can then command it so.

Looking at life in a purely energetic way, the energy of our spirit is light, but a very special frequency of light. We are eternal light. I know some may differ with me on that, especially if religion enters the discussion, but when I had a near-death experience, I was surrounded in this incredible light that is unforgettable. Clairaudiently, I knew by feeling a connection to One that the death-rebirth cycle is eternal, just like when stars explode and we say they 'die', their energy goes into making another planet, star, or galaxy. While we have a connection to each other on this planet, our connections go well beyond our three-dimensional living plane. There are millions upon millions that already know this -- not only those of us living on this planet that have already experienced something similar or have just "known" through higher connections that they are eternal, but also all those souls that have passed on while you and I have continued to live in this multi-dimensional space on earth, many dimensions of which are around us but of which we cannot readily see or feel unless we are more finely attuned to them. For example, someone that has died (aka moved consciously beyond our three-dimensional world) recently could still be connecting to you or someone else in this three-dimensional plane. Yes, that communication exists – only you are taught to deny its existence – but your Higher Self never denies you the truth of the reality you seek. Of course, going back to societal 'norms', we have been 'taught' (i.e., programmed) that we are to be afraid of spirits or ghosts, and that we are crazy if we believe in loved ones coming to talk to us. Oh no, you are not cracked or lunatic, you are indeed 'waking-up' into sensing other new dimensional fields.

The Awakening Is About Combining Mathematical Knowledge & Spiritual Intelligence

Institutions of higher learning that break-away from the Establishment's 'old' and moldy roots of lies and corrupt knowledge will delve into Cerebral Energetics (mentioned earlier in the book).

Old news is that famous scientists with IQs of more than 190 (of which, in so-called theory, only 1 person in 1 billion has) have more or less speculated multiple dimensions (up to 13). But this is not about having high IQ. The new awakening is clear when it says this is the time to gain on spiritual intelligence, not necessarily on mathematical knowledge. But I say that because the universe is all so cleverly and amusingly devised on mathematics, it is good to grow first the spiritual intelligence, catch it up to the mathematical knowledge we have, then advance both realms.

The combination of spirituality and mathematics is very likely to be taught in 'advanced-thinking' universities and other educational places around the globe as this awakening is further aroused by the uplifting but volatile vibrations that are going to continue to stream into our galactic plane in coming years causing massive amounts of change – more conversions, adjustments and transformation in general than the human species has ever been through. So, don't begin to program yourself to "get used" to adaptation; instead program yourself to sync-in and enjoy the adaptation process – this way you will channel-in abundance instead of struggle to keep-up.

I do believe that we will soon see a major paradigm shift in consciousness occur. This will very likely include acceptance of people connecting to departed loved ones. For some it will only take a small nudge in someone (even myself as half a stranger in your life) saying, "I accept you for telling me that you can connect with your deceased mother or daughter." For others, it may take a close buddy or someone who is very trusted, to say, "Ya know, I had this amazing experience, and I can't explain it, but I saw my [passed-on] mother in front of me, and she was saying..." To which the friend or minister, for example, may ask, "Wait a sec bud / dear friend, your mother passed away last year, and you're now telling me she was standing there in front of you!?" Replicate this conversation a thousand times and then those thousand people tell another twenty people, and soon,

before long, you have a new vibration on the planet with acceptance of 'seeing' or hearing departed loved souls. The sun's shift in magnetic and energetic streams / wavelengths will be one factor in coming years to help or even force this shift in consciousness.

Go Internally To Find Your Purpose

Look, I have to say something else that is going to help so many look internally to find peace and spirituality, rather than our programmed society telling us that we have to focus on finding our purpose, our needs and other goals in other places. What I am getting at is this: there are so many "lost" souls out there -- in our three-dimensional world. They do not know their purpose. Perhaps you are one of those souls that is searching, not knowing where to go or look. Do you really know what you are here to do?

Well, here is an answer: go internally. Begin this connection process to Divine. Don't feel the need to jump on the high horse of any religion if you are not religious. Even if you are religious, but are not finding God in life, the answer is to connect first internally and then command your internal travel to the Divine (a non-being of just benevolent Light). You might think I'm speaking in riddles, but piece apart the sentences. What am I saying to you?

God As An Energy Flow In The Highest Realm

You are a God-Self. You are a part of Source, of One. Do you understand that? I mean, truly, energetically, do you get that? God loves you because you are a part of God. God does not hate you because you did something wrong or bad. You are connected to Source, to Buddha, One, Muhammad, and any other deity, Divine Being, or person that you feel connected to. Even though there were (are) certain individuals that were (are) advanced souls, what I refer to as one and of the same is the Connected Love that makes us One Source Code.

There is no deity that is going to zap you down because you did something wrong. There IS the law of attraction which says that you will magnetize energy of that which you produce internally and that which you provide outside Self: so if you do something that is bad energetically ... say you intentionally kill a grasshopper, by picking it apart, like I knew some guy that was so twisted that he not only enjoyed doing this but also liked showing others how to do it, and even did it in front of children watching him (nauseating madman!), you are making, creating and enveloping an energetic vibration that will bring back more negativity into your life.

See, in religion, we all personify: most call God a man, and then we fight over whether God could be a woman. It is so silly. As the awakening on our planet happens, as we stream toward a higher level of multi-dimensional consciousness, we won't need to argue about whether God is masculine or feminine. God is an energy flow in the highest realm. If you wish to personify a bit, you might want to add that God is the most evolved spirit, and since you and I are each a God-Self, a part of the total universe of Light, we are connected in so many energetic ways with a purpose to spread love, compassion and kindness, and to spread insights and ideas to help others you meet on your Living Pathway. That essentially is part of the meaning of life as expressed earlier.

THE ESTABLISHMENT WANTS DIFFERENCES IN RELIGION TO ADVANCE ITS MILITARY INDUSTRIAL COMPLEX

If we stopped arguing about which religion is best in our world (a pathway which is all supported by the Military Industrial Complex), we would stop most of our war-like attitudes against each other. Just remember that you are one of One, a self of God-Self, and are a part of flow in Universal Streaming Consciousness. Once you have that inside you, you inch toward peace, and then, only then, can you see and realize your purpose in life.

The Establishment wants to have so many differences in religion. The Establishment wants to separate human beings based upon different religious teachings so they can increase their war agenda and cause more misery and less freedom in the world. In other words, part of the Agenda is to have "man fight man", and for us to wage holy war against each other. It is all a part of their perverse agenda. One of the biggest goals of the Establishment is to advance the Military Industrial Complex, and this includes not just bombs and guns but mind control technologies and other weaponry that sends out frequencies that incite people to turn on each other.

Move Away From Establishment & Connect To Source

The Establishment does not want you knowing that in energetic terms, some woman in Syria could be your sister energy, or some guy in Nigeria is part of your human vibration. They don't want you reacting in love to each other, because that increases the population of the planet. The Establishment wants eugenics systems in place: they have publicly advocated for de-population.

History repeats itself so often: this time, as technology is going to new levels of evil, what you don't hear and what you are not told is that the true research goals are to gain control of the understanding of the energetic and spiritual worlds combined, described above and then limit humankind's advancement at the level of entering multiple dimensions (through mental abilities and accessing information from energies that enter and exit our chakras).

The Establishment wants to promote eugenics, weaponry and other negative influences: they essentially bow down to Luciferian principles and are sown into huge negative karmic cycles. Of course some won't believe this: they will call it nonsense. But do the research: see the "clubs" that the elite pedal amongst themselves. See the child abduction and slavery rings that they control – of which excellent research and journalism has 'broken'.

Move away from the Establishment and their different promulgations. You will suddenly see so much Abundance come into your life once you 'rebirth' yourself energetically to realize that you can make it on your own, and you don't need all the hand-out's that enslave you deeper into the System. The Establishment wants you on the System 'payroll' so they can easily control you – your movements, your thoughts, your activities, your "everything". And once you are 'hooked', you are essentially a 21st-century slave to the System.

When you connect to Source, you raise your individual flow in Universal consciousness; you not only become, you feel, a greater part of the Big Picture. To me, it doesn't matter whether you go to church, a mosque, or you simply sit upon volcanic lava rock and close your eyes. What does matter is that you go inward, commanding connection to Divine or Source to raise your own awareness and ultimately to help the planet move forward in a positive way. Doing this innermost growing will reap rewards beyond anything you might have experienced so far in life.

Remember, your inner be-ing or God-Self can connect with your Higher Self or One / God / Source. One of my favorite things to do every few days is to reflect into the amazing space beyond me, beyond our planet, and contemplate the bigger questions of 'where am I truly from?', and 'where is my soul going to after I end my Earth Walk?'

This wonderful self-talk to Divine Energy actually is a way to increase the positive vibrations in my cells. No wonder the field of metaphysics (with gurus like Dr. Wayne Dyer, Louise Hay, Gregg Braden, and others) is teaching us to step beyond the actual consciousness of our day. My main message is that once you connect to the ultimate consciousness of the Universe – everything from watching a spider build its web to witnessing a 'shooting star' or an aurora – you actually elevate your conscious mind, and then you can actually 'lift-off' to travel multi-dimensionally. You don't need a spaceship to go to Sirius to see the origins of dolphins. You can mind-voyage, otherwise known as astral travel or go on a stellar journey. The CIA once had a program called Stargate where it trained people to be able to locate different objects on Mars. It's called Remote Viewing (RV), and is all alive in multiple government programs today. So before someone labels me 'nuts' for mentioning something that is outside a certain comfort zone, I urge that person to do their homework and see what the government is doing to gain the advantage – the gain to be controlling us, the 'regular' population, the slaves-to-be. Once you know more, then you have the advantage. If you can 'curve' events through Mind Transformation Energy (MTE), then those elite systems are far less likely to 'grab' onto you and 'lock' you into place. If someone is reading this saying, "Yeah, man, whatever ...", then that person is already morphing into a zombie (and of course that specific word is used by FEMA and other government agencies). They know a zombie was once a human but due to a frequency shift in the brain, the cognizant thinking pattern has shifted to a lower-evolved state such that s/he is now much more easily controlled (to the benefit of the System under the Elite Agenda).

Open your mind -- go beyond the programming, and learn once and for all, how to have the life you truly deserve, full of abundance.

You could always wait until your next lifetime, but for me, there is no time like the Now.

The biggest takeaway here is that you can lift yourself up so high, higher than your current realm of spirituality, or so much higher than perhaps the cauldron you find yourself hitting too regularly, and empower your direction in this karmic lifetime by commanding an open channel with cosmic guidance. It can be done: it is a padlock that literally all human be-ings can unlock, just know that the key is believing in the change you can master to plug-in to your God-given right of connecting to your origin. Once you have done this, energetically, you are then attracting the full stream of abundance in all its glory. You're darn right this is going to make you think: in fact, it's very possible I am just getting warmed-up, especially once you hit Volume 2 and beyond. I have to build-up the concepts and new thought pattern, otherwise it's like throwing you into a doctorate degree program when you're 10 years old.

The opposite to gaining abundance is being 'lost' on this earthly planet, and having no idea what your purpose is because you have lost or never recognized your connection to Divine. Being connected to Source and knowing your God-Self is the most fulfilling thing I have been able to accomplish, other than being chosen as a father by my two children, Skye and Gaia ... the Skyaia® team (and now you know the other meaning). By the way, my children will often tell me about their most recent origin, with no prodding or whispered suggestions. Skye tells me he is from Sirius where he talks about his interactions with the dolphin homeland, and he tells me he remembers traveling a long way to get to Earth. Gaia talks about being new to Earth.

The Disconnection Between Vaccinations & A Heavenly Connection

Although we will get to this in a later chapter (and say even more in Volume 2), it is a crying shame how the overwhelming majority of children these days are vaccinated to the hilt, with overdoses that are criminal, because there is overwhelming evidence that they cause behavioral / emotional shifts, mental dumbing-down, or worse – as in vaccinations maim or kill. But these poisonous vaccinations, loaded with toxins and even nanotechnology now, interrupt our stream of consciousness, and cancel out the innate – yes, the instinctive ability to connect inter-dimensionally and merge one's vibration with Divine. But that is the utterly repulsive goal of the Elite: they don't want "Cute Sarah" (age 3) or "Handsome George" (age 7) remembering their Light Source, nor do they want them questioning too much.

Let me say that again: vaccinations of TODAY are a tool of the Establishment that limit one's connection to the Divine. In this regard, I say with avid confirmation that vaccinations are just another tool in the medical bag of a Luciferian-worshipping doctor. Let me put it bluntly: ONCE a doctor knows the horrible number of poisons in the average vaccination, that doctor is not going to give those vaccinations to children, and IF that doctor does, then that doctor is not praying to God; that doctor is connecting to the so-called Underworld in a religious sense.

In the 1960s and 1970s, most vaccinations did not have all the poisons that they have today. I have done my research: I will show you in another part of Skyaia® all the contaminated and harmful stuff in an average vaccination. You will be shocked. And to think that most doctors claim ignorance on this subject is a crime in and of itself. Vaccinations, as physical immunity suppressors and mental blockers to higher levels of consciousness, are all a part of the programming: governments (and even some of the most powerful corporations that manufacture these poisons) are more than well-acquainted with the ideological evil pursuits of sequestering (as in "repossessing") our deepest abilities to connect to higher realms. By not allowing this process to happen, they are literally making human be-ings into un-conscious slaves (or zombies). Aside, later in the health chapters (or in the blog), I will provide a Medical Exemption form to give to your doctor so that you never have to take vaccinations again. These days, it takes a special doctor to sign the Medical Waiver, but it can be done with perseverance.

The conflict is one that is fortunately in its infantile stage: there is still hope that as more parents awaken, they do not give these venomous inoculations to the ones they so dearly love, thereby granting them more freedom at the energetic plane of existence. As more parents cease vaccinating, we are winning the war against the Medical Nazi Poisoning of this era.

Part 2
CONNECT TO SKYAIA®

Chapter 8

Your Path Is The Key

From Our Cells To The Cosmos, Everything Is Energy

"SOMETHING WENT *TERRIBLY WRONG* BETWEEN *DESIGN* AND *DEVELOPMENT*."

The 'big picture' of life is absolutely huge. If you 'get' this big picture, you are evolving, advancing, receiving abundance in many different ways, you are usually joyful knowing that you can command your life in the direction you want, and you know or at least want to know how to guard yourself from the infiltrating forces of the underworld. Your path is the key: if you concentrate on Self (you), without believing the negativities of what other people believe and say about you, then you are so more free to accomplish the things you have come here to do.

However, if you keep your mind closed, your mouth shut, turn a blind eye to the big picture of life, and listen to those pushing you around in life against your intuition and dreams, you will unfortunately suffer, you will be controlled, and you will feel on many days as though your life is an ever-present death sentence. This is the choice. This is the blunt reality, and the so-called duality.

Block Negative Energies & Command Positive Energies

The big picture requires you wake-up and take the path to freedom, or go back to sleep and be controlled. We all have the choice. Therefore, the big picture is all about your will, your determination, your ability to truly separate dark from light, and becoming empowered to make truly insightful decisions to benefit your life and others you love and care about.

The big picture is about the energies that surround you. Much of this is at first invisible, but as you train yourself to become more aware, and as you align to positive forces, new dimensional fields will slowly appear to you.

You and I are energy. We are a shell of bones, flesh, blood, water, and so much more. We have a number of electrical systems including a heart (in which even in the early 1960s, scientists found that a biomagnetic field projected from the human heart, and now of course we test any heart issue with an electrocardiogram); and, we have a mind (which pulses electricity across synaptic junctions). We have magnetoreceptors (to sense magnetic fields), and medical science has proven that geomagnetism affects the light system in our eyes. The human body produces an electromagnetic field, more strongly generated by our heart, brain, nervous system, glands and even skin. I call this energy our Bio-Electromagnetic Field Spectrum (BEMFS), and I have observed this field mostly around my head, ear lobes, palms and feet, where the body has more nerve connection ends. Yogis, yoga instructors, those that meditate, and numerous others are discovering more about this, which is adequately documented even in "Western-based" science and medical journals. It's just that so much is never brought in front of us.

Weather is not just clouds, sunshine, wind and precipitation. Weather is energy: ever-flowing, ever-morphing, always adapting. The sun, our stars, the cosmos ... it is all energy. Even the myriad of cycles are energetically connected in some amazingly intricate web. Weather is not just the cold fronts, low pressure systems, and airmasses that you see depicted on the average weather forecast; weather is all about distinguishing "magnetic pulses" that vibrate and change the energy fields to produce the weather.

Science is measuring the human energy field, and in a few decades mainstream science has gone from an assurance that there is no such thing as an energy field around the human body to an absolute certainty that it exists. Moreover, we are readily understanding the roles of energy fields in not only health and disease, but also in climate. Unfortunately, advanced understanding of electromagnetics is quickly being sought by the Military Industrial Complex to improve capabilities in weaponry. Many people are simply not aware of the importance of energy in all its forms, yet just as many people are waking-up to realize that energetic therapies can take their appropriate place in clinical medicine just like if we think outside the box we can better understand our climate patterns through the study of atmospheric electromagnetics and even best comprehend the importance of cosmic energy for our own survival.

The great discoveries, past and present and future, including ones I share with you in this book from scientific analysis, research, and even dreams, and altered states will give us a deeper understanding of the energy of life, the energy of dis-ease, the energy of healing, the energy of climate aberrations, and the energy of alien life and even the true origin of human life.

Ultimately, in searching for the ultimate mystery of life, we need to have a more complete understanding of energy, both from the inner working of our cells to the huge power of stars birthing in the cosmos. This is just one reason why this book is called 'Skyaia®' – 'Sky', from the cosmos to 'Gaia', our Mother Earth, joined together makes 'Sky' + 'Gaia' = Skyaia®. All energy is connected in some shape or form. And once we better understand the amazing energetic 'magic' of life to one, two, three or more levels above the three-dimensional plane toward the amazing concepts of dimensional-creationism and the true purpose of humanity, then and only then can we escape from the 'dead' course set upon us by those that wish to control our bodies, our minds, our thinking, and even our ability to astral project into other dimension. The human race must literally become the free energies we are destined to be. If we are enslaved at the cerebral level by the controlling forces that shadow so many governments and other parts of the Establishment (review the definition at the beginning of the book), then the human race will suffer tremendously for many decades.

As you may have already surmised, energetic vibration is huge: much of it involves electromagnetics, of which humans are just beginning to learn about because they realize that an understanding of electromagnetics and energetics in general is the overwhelming source of command that provides abundance in all different ways in life. Energetic vibrations encompass literally everything, from one end of life to the other, from cellular immunity to weapons of death, from the planet's climate system to cosmic forces, from transport of Self into a different dimension to the development of pre-crime (coming to a city near you sooner than you think; see the movie "Minority Report"). Energetics contains two sides, like Ying and Yang: dark and light. This book will show you both sides. In solving future challenges that face humanity in months to decades to come, we must all choose the side of Light and be ready for the ever-increasing temptations from the dark because as the new dimensions come closer to Earth (that which cannot be seen through the public / research telescopes that the population knows about), the vibrations of both Light and Dark will intensify, causing more and more chaotic interactions in society.

As the spectrum of natural light shifts on Earth, one of the biggest challenges as a society will be the effects of this change on our mental and emotional and physical faculties. Since our brains and bodies are optimized on a certain magnetic vibration and an unwavering frequency of life, when there is a shift, we will surely notice. However, we may not be able to explain to each other why this is happening. Due to the different 'play' of the light and vibration on our minds, the inability for so many to avoid depression is one of these challenges. The way to avoid this potential depressive state is to sleep more. Sleeping 'reboots' your natural system and connection to One, the energy that connects us all when we sleep. Now that this shift is accelerating to the point where an increasing number can truly feel it, if you continue to be a super-Mom/Pop or a business ladder title-worshipping workaholic, you are much more likely to see the negative effects of a depressive state enter your be-ing.

Now is the time to enter a balance in life by attaining the philosophy of work-smart and rejuvenating / recharging your spiritual batteries. This does not mean you should necessarily become a maharishi, but it does mean that you might want to do a self-check of your path and realize whether or not you are on a path of self-destruction.

At this point, permit me to sidetrack on something that has happened to a lot of us in life in one circumstance or another – even as adults – and that is bullying – and it comes in many forms such as discrimination, victimization, intimidation, harassment, oppression and even persecution. I am going to guarantee you that some will ridicule me for my educational accomplishments and beliefs. Remember, you can never please everyone. As you know so far, I proclaim in doing many things differently. I have never gone down the proverbial Main Street to learn what I am sharing with you in this book. Why would I?

Do you think you can really find the truth by jockeying up with most at Big Pharma Central that have learned nothing but to bully, lie and cause problems to those that don't follow the same philosophy?

Of course not.

ADULT BULLYING SACRIFICES MANY DREAMS FOR TOO MANY PEOPLE

An increasing number of people that want to get into medicinal fields do not have much cash saved-up or they don't want to be indentured servants to the banks for the rest of their lives. While quite a few who want to pursue medicine have a large amount of cash in a bank account, many take huge loans in the hundreds of thousands of dollars that literally become very burdensome to pay back, especially because they just keep on amassing new and bigger loans as their practice gets larger and/or their X-ray rooms keep expanding.

Many allopathic doctors will make fun of you if you don't go to some Ivy-League school of medicine. In fact, there is so much hostile competition within a unit of allopathic medicine, namely inside a hospital or a larger practice. It is apparently just awful on many levels, so I have heard from genuine sources.

So it should come as no surprise to imagine the fun poked at me for doing a double doctorate (a PhD in the USA, and a DSc in India), a path that some allopaths or those aligned to Mainstream ways might call 'maverick'. Permit me to tell you about it. I tell you because, like I said before, I am open-book. And I have an important message to all those out there that have dreams to assist the world, but feel intimidated to act upon them for fear of being ridiculed or hated or even worse.

I had a first goal in the study of healing and truth, not to prescribe Big Pharma medicine. I also had a second goal not to become in debt. I also had the third goal to think out of the box – to gain new insights and to share that knowledge with the public. I did not want to spread the increasing conflict between energy of darkness in the field of well-being (too much of the allopathic world of corruption, power, control surrounding most medical issues and putting a Band-Aid on the source of the problem), and energy of lightness in well-being (the naturopathic world of digging to the root of the cause, and soldering together the natural intelligence of the body with ancient therapies of health-giving). I had the goal to gain new perspective by seeking a global education, and namely in this case, to go back to the roots of where naturopathic medicine began many centuries ago – to India. In addition, I wanted to continue my career in climate science at the same time in studying naturopathic medicine, and to essentially have an institution of learning that was open to hearing about my collaborative ideas in seeing how the studies of climate and health could be joined together at not just a physical level but at an energetic (aka electromagnetic) level, especially seeing as the planet's climate is proven to be influential at a magnetic and electrical level (namely everything from lightning and severe storms to the solar wind). Lastly, at the time, I had the fourth goal to not have to disrupt my life and my family by moving outside of Montana, a place where I thrived mentally and physically due to the incredibly positive electromagnetics (of course, that was all before the Fukushima Daiichi reactor catastrophe, which is going to be a real game-changer in life in the United States of America). In my heart, I want to lead by example, especially in helping to guide many people who are wanting to study an advanced degree but do not know how to do so. I welcome you to get in touch if you are interested in following a similar path in "new-wave" science and/or natural / energy medicine.

A few times in my life, I was told by potentially influential people not to follow my share dreams. My life would have been much different, for the worse, if I had listened to those people. So for all those out there that are interested in higher learning, especially in science and natural health, I tell you the following story so that you too will not make a potential mistake by listening to others who may not have your best interests in mind. It is so important not to have someone else 'approve' what s/he wants you to learn. Reverse this. Dream up what you want to study, then find an institution of higher learning that is open to and pleased to have you join them. This is the first and most important step of collaborative positivity rather than negative control. Any degree, especially a masters or doctorate, must be all about customization and developing your own path, and in doing so, the 'right' center of higher learning will see your journey set forth as a meaningful way to advance your interest, whether it be naturopathic medicine, climate science or any other subject to theoretically help the world. If you don't get that feeling, intuitively or otherwise, from that place of higher learning, then distance yourself from that entity.

I attained my Ph.D. in Natural Health (with a collaborative effort in how climate affects our well-being on an energetic perspective) from a well-known school called Clayton College of Natural Health (CCNH). This school achieved over 30,000 graduates, many who have written other books in natural health and new ways of healing, some becoming quite famous due to their good work and popularity with clients all over the world. I was so disappointed that this school closed its doors in 2010

after thirty years in business. Some now say that this makes my degree less useful or even that it invalidates my achievement. This is of course pure rubbish. Since 2010, I have also had some messages mainly from those tied to allopathic areas that have told me that CCNH was a mail-order program. This is nothing further from the truth. I studied for six years and seven months to get that Ph.D. degree: I took over 20 courses and did a dissertation.

So why I am telling you this? For three reasons: first, I am open-book; second, sometimes, stuff happens in life that you never expected, like the bankruptcy of your graduate degree school. Second, through easy research, you will find that Birmingham, Alabama (where CCNH was located) was the first largest municipal bankruptcy in the United States, before of course Detroit 'fell'. And sadly, due to the incredible debt levels in the USA and the failing economic policies that are affecting many cities at this time, there will be other schools and institutions of higher learning that go unfortunately to the wayside due to the huge debts in many poorly financially-managed cities of America. And third – and most important – because many will tell you not to do something even though you subliminally feel it is following your dream, it is incredibly important to listen to your intuition, your guiding light, and the source of that connection that knows you best.

For me, I could have attended any university in the world for doctoral graduate work (due to my Ivy-League Cornell University undergraduate degree, my International MBA, my Assistant Professor positions at both Hawaii Pacific University and University of Montana – Billings, and other qualifications), as long as I forked over the incredibly high rates of tuition. But I realized it was not about HOW it would look like to others, or WHAT others thought of that piece of paper called the diploma; I instead realized it was about what I could achieve and give to the world to make it a better place. I had to follow my passion, and if another professor wasn't on-board and I had to sacrifice part of my dream, I wasn't going to do it. I got out of ego and did something that I was truly passionate about. That is one of the most important "bottom lines" in life, especially in education and your career.

Some still believe that getting an education by maximizing the benefits of technology is still not accepted. The changing of the guard from the old to the new has always been something challenged, but I do not need the 'approval' of someone telling me what is good or isn't good. In fact, if you want a good mantra in your life right now, here is a 'Simon Says' line that I positively empower in your life at this time:

> "I am my own individual Self be-ing. My life is not sculpted by the needs and opinions of others. I bless all in my life, and I welcome all Abundance on my Path in doing what my soul, heart and mind deem the best for my spirit. And so it is. Namasté." If you feel any of this applies to you, write down that incredibly powerful mantra, and watch it change the way you react to the indoctrination that has tried to or has stopped you in your tracks.

What I gained in my studies at CCNH is in my brain. Similar to life, people (and even family members) and other places will come and go in your lifetime, but the reward(s) are always the things you learn and keep as memories and experiences: that is the key. Like I said earlier, at the time when CCNH ceased operations, the City of Birmingham, Alabama (where CCNH was located) was going through municipal bankruptcy proceedings, the largest ever in the United States. Due to this burgeoning economic recession, there had been a decrease in new student CCNH enrollment, and perhaps fewer students were paying in full like I did in 2004. Maybe CCNH management had spent too much in expanding too fast, similar to the fate of many well-intentioned businesses that become very successful? Even though this whole event made me evaluate more the themes in life of impermanence and the fragility of an economic downturn, of course I wonder if it was more than just this. There is a main suspicion that CCNH had become so increasingly popular, that it was becoming a threat to Big Pharma. Maybe Big Pharma may have decided to throw its dinosaur weight around, and pull some formula of corruption out of its big poisonous hole such that it said, 'We'll give [the top three members of the CCNH Board] five million dollars each on collapsing the School.'. CCNH was in a process of getting its accreditation, and things had never looked so rosy, so its ending was very suspicious. In summary, there could have been, and likely was more than one reason for the School's downfall, but one thing was for sure – it was a place of learning that was on the cutting-edge of energy medicine, which is the future of so much healing in decades ahead. And I am still proud to be one of its graduates, no matter what someone may say to the contrary.

My Doctor of Science (DSc), from the Indian Board of Alternative Medicines [IBAM], was all about this continued dream to pursue something that I was passionate in understanding from the base of my heart to the central core of my scientific and theoretical thinking. I have introduced the new field of biometeoelectromagnetics, and it has helped many people already. It combines the study of meteorology (meteo), health / life (bio) and the electromagnetics from magnetic interferences in the cosmos and the magnetosphere of our planet to the electrical stimulations inside our brains and magnetic lines in our auric sphere surrounding our body.

Let me say that the huge irony is that there is becoming so much demand (from the public) of naturopathic / energy doctors but there are not that many well-funded schools that provide degrees in advanced alternative medicine. Of course, this is changing, but there is, like I just alluded to above, a big wave of jealousy, resentment and distrust from schools of allopathic medicine and Big Pharma directed at the growth of the incredible awakening of a mass population hearing about and discovering the wonderful benefits of naturopathic medicine. Countries like Germany operate a large part of their medical disciplines in the naturopathic / homeopathic areas, and it has been an incredible success. Now, with more and more Americans getting sick to death of doctors spending five minutes or less with them, and being given prescriptions that "order" them to take medicine with terrible side effects, people are turning more and more to the multiple disciples across natural healing.

Big Pharma and related pill-popping (control) "medicine" is feeling threatened in a very big way. But as long as the People speak with their wallet, their voice and their ballot, Big Pharma will have to morph and combine their work with the side of medicine that is better 'understood' by the intricacies of the human body – natural medicine – so that we can prosper from better healing for mind, body and soul.

CHAPTER 9

THE CLIMATE CHANGE SCAM

How Carbon Dioxide Is Synonymous With Taxation & Control

In the past, there have been absolutely monumental climate shifts. Ice core and oceanic records show that there have been at least half a dozen rapid cooling periods in the past 750,000 years. Some of them were due to incredibly explosive volcanoes, especially multiple eruptions at the same time or within a small span of years blocking out sunlight due to tremendous amounts of gases and/or ash in the atmosphere. Some of these abrupt climate changes were due to asteroids, similarly causing a large shield of dust to take months or years to re-settle. And, as other climate scientists will attest, those especially outside the government-sponsored grants (the ones that force scientists to choose between signing their name to garbage or not receiving a paycheck to keep their families in lower middle income neighborhoods) or liberal university press, some of the climate aberrations have been due to cosmic magnetic interferences which have initially caused a micro wobble on the Earth's axis which has then caused a myriad of inner processes that are finely-balanced or tuned to become erratic.

What Really Scares Me Is Technology-Caused Global Cooling

In cutting to the chase, given the extent of the government brainwashing, there are going to be a lot of non-believers when I say that carbon dioxide has a negligible effect on global climate. If you want to talk about anthropogenic global climate shifts, look up HAARP, sonar and other technologies that use electromagnetics, like EMP (Electro Magnetic Pulse) weaponry. These have been governed by minds that may on the surface be brilliant to some, but don't let looks and abilities fool you. Those working in the

Military Industrial Complex, those citizens lacking integrity that get paychecks from the government and other large corporations to help make weapons, and people who give no thought to the fact that each day they are helping indirectly to cause more hatred and suffering on our planet, are way too dense intellectually and spiritually to comprehend that the overwhelming cause of any human-caused temperature or precipitation extremes are done not by carbon dioxide but through modification of energetic vibrations.

It is very important to bring up carbon dioxide yet again because I want you to see how ludicrous the brainwashing not only has become but how insane it may become before we get leaders that reverse all the madness and we, as a society, come to our senses.

There is irrefutable scientific evidence that Earth was actually warmer 1,000 years ago. Of course, you might see so-called "verification" from those trying to pull the wool over your eyes for political or personal gain that this was not the case, but I can tell you with extremely high confidence that the data from this other side of the table is not scientific. There was actually less ice in the Arctic 6,000 years ago, and I don't remember any major factories back then, do you? The levels of carbon dioxide are actually the same today as when the planet was warmer than today, the same 1,000 years ago. This means that the natural cycles are overwhelmingly (at least close to 90% of the entire equation, to be conservative, if not higher) the cause of climate shifts. There are normal fluctuations in the 'big picture' (i.e., cosmic) level of carbon dioxide levels.

You know what *really* scares me? Not the idiots in their pulpits that have no science background and then spout-off their panic about the climate versus economy agenda. Not any temperature rises ... because to tell you the truth, I would personally love to see the globe get warmer. It would be fantastic for the overwhelming majority of the population; we'd surely have a higher abundance of crops (of course, not throwing into the equation the corrupt Monsanto's of the world putting wrenches into the mix). Oh no, what really scares me is the combination of natural global cooling AND the asinine process of climate geo-engineering whereby leaders authorize spraying of microscopic / nano particles which act as mirrors that reflect back sunlight. If THIS happens, then we'll be in for a dangerous Ice Age, especially if this all hits at the same time as Solar Cycle 25, which peaks in about 2014. The reason why the "next" solar cycle (we are peaking into Cycle 24 as this book is being published, with each cycle lasting an approximate 11 years, give or take a couple to a few on each side in the minority of cycles) is important is because NASA and scientists like myself have calculated that the solar sunspots could -- with high confidence (above 80 percent!) -- be so low, that they could match the low number of sunspots that occurred in the Dalton Minimum (approximately 1790 to 1830), a period on the climate timescale that brought extensive cold to the planet (and we know this not only from records in Europe, and historical accords from the USA, but also paleontological evidence from tree rings, ice cores, pollen yields in sedimentation layers, oxygen isotopic analysis and so much more. Now the Dalton period also had a higher number of erupting volcanoes. While the so-called "year without a summer" (1816) happened just over half-way into the Dalton Minimum, it is likely of course that a significant reason for this colder era was because of the eruption of Indonesia's Tambora, which was easily one of, if not, the largest volcanic eruption since Christ walked the earth. But there is much evidence to show that low sunspot activity triggers more volcanoes to erupt. That catalyst, in my scientific opinion, is electromagnetic. So, rewind the tape and see that my theory, based upon much technical substantiation, is the sun started the process, and in its lower sunspot cycle, which then caused the sun to give off less heat, it also sent 'communication' to Earth in the form of decreased electromagnetics, of which in order to "make up" the difference, the Earth then had to "pump-out" higher electromagnetics, which then activated more volcanoes, which then further cooled the planet. See, it's so cool: it's all related, and the Earth and even the solar system, have a method to regulate different parameters naturally. Who do WE think we are to think egotistically that we make such a huge difference when in reality, the entire human race is the weight of but a mere speck of sand compared to the importance of natural cycles representing the heaviness of all sand on all beaches in the world (and probably much more).

Now let me go back to anthropogenic global warming (AGW) and say this very succinctly: climate change caused by humans is not what you think. We are told that because of our carbon dioxide -- the gas that we breathe out -- the gas that has been termed 'evil' by the scam of an agency called the Environmental Protection Agency (EPA), a bureau of incompetence in which the only thing they are protecting is their own butts with blood-stained paychecks -- we are making the temperature climb significantly. This is like saying that because there are more African Americans than Caucasians in jails in the United States, that African Americans are more predisposed to violence. Both of these statements are absolutely bogus. If African-Americans were given equal opportunities, and if we as a society realized more that money and programs centering around loving each other more and family values (instead of giving that same money, and more, to countries that use the dough to build weapons that then tear apart our families years down the line), we would not have this immense problem of more African Americans in jail.

Perhaps the world Establishment has purposefully confused the global populace – that otherwise would wish to unite together to better protect ourselves against the course of climate change – in order to appear a more mighty leader in showing they can save the planet. In this accusation, there is evidence that Establishment organizations purposefully changed true data with the intent to meet their own political and economic plans, and in the process "sacrificed" a few individuals here and there by embarrassing them and ending their careers, of course after ordering them to fudge the data. Their trickery goes to extreme lengths.

That previous argument was valid because I cannot stand it when I am lied to in my face. As a scientist, I am constantly lied to, even by other atmospheric scientists that are hopelessly brainwashed and haven't delved into higher 'bigger picture' sciences like energetics: they will tell me that they believe carbon dioxide is the root cause of most of warming cycles on the planet since the Industrial Revolution began. There are some real brainiacs out there that know more than a few things about earth science, but when it comes to their ability to see a bigger picture and the fact that our planet has been much warmer, even in the last few thousand years, compared with today, without there being any factories or x number of billion people breathing carbon dioxide back then, they end-up with a flunking grade.

Fortunately, there are many scientists on the side of this book – that blaming carbon dioxide on global warming is a complete swindle of humanity in peddling-back our economic progress.

Many Layers Of Wool Are Being Pulled Over Our Eyes

The planet has 'meridian lines' of energy and when we blast a billion volts of electricity into the ionosphere, or we resonate huge volumes of sound in the oceanic trenches, we actually alter the earth's electromagnetic imbalance. I won't disrespect you by saying that you may not be able to comprehend this, but I will say that you need to educate readers that want logical and scientific answers. Think out of the box. There have been at least 75 temperature shifts, naturally occurring, in the last 4500 years. Much of this was due to solar dynamics, volcanoes, and naturally shifting electromagnetics.

But, when the brilliant sunlight streams positively across the valley of logic, when most see that we have entered a global cooling period (again, similar to the one in the 1970s), and there are more near-future examples of agricultural protectionism because more countries are witnessing more intense weather disasters (due also to the technological innovations like HAARP that have gone crooked), then there is going to be a lot of back-pedaling and even jailing those that lied with full intent to make profit on climate scams. And let me add this: there is oodles of scientific evidence to show this cooling pattern in complete contrast to NASA (and AGW followers) announcing that 2009, 2010, 2011, 2012 and so forth was the quote-unquote hottest year on record. Maybe these people should actually take a class in knowing the difference between taking their own rectal temperature and measuring the atmospheric conditions with instrumentation that is away from airport runways or inner city factory exhaust fans! Still, with people that have their heads up their asses, how can one possibly expect them to see the discrepancy, especially when they see nothing wrong in stirring their coffee after they pull their thermometer out from the loose lips of their sphincters that do all their talking for them!

It is unfortunate to have to tell you that the Establishment will very likely continue their ploy of the carbon cycle "science" even though it will be false, misleading, and corrupt. But it will bring in billions of revenue from the peasants (you and I) to the elite (Establishment coffers).

I have inferred that the difference in the thinking from future candidates for public office in the world's leading "democracies" is going to make a gigantic difference for how it will impact you and me. If we see a set of major natural disasters in the short-term, this difference will be even more important.

It is also of paramount importance that more of the media embrace true science and stop pedaling the same lies that governments are handing them to distribute. It is not true when the report on the television or a news brief on the radio says, "most scientists believe that we must stop global warming." This is old news. In fact, it's just the opposite: many eminent scientists, far more renowned than myself, agree that global warming caused by carbon dioxide is a complete and utter farce.

I still brim cheek to cheek when I remember reading about Nobel Prize-winning physicist Ivar Giaever who publicly resigned from the APS (American Physical Society). In that letter, he wrote, "I did not renew because I cannot live with the statement (from the APS): 'The evidence is incontrovertible: Global warming is occurring. If no mitigating actions are taken, significant disruptions in the Earth's physical and ecological systems, social systems, security and human health are likely to occur. We must reduce emissions of greenhouse gases beginning now.' Dr. Giaever continued his writing: "In the APS it is okay to discuss whether the mass of the proton changes over time and how a multi-universe behaves, but the evidence of global warming is incontrovertible?" This was absolutely sensational!

And to this day, I am not a part of the AMS (American Meteorological Society) because they openly display such rubbish and subscribe to junk science about global warming and carbon dioxide as the culprit of most of it. In fact, I wrote to the AMS director, and of course nothing came of it, but perhaps with this publication, they will have to re-think their strategy as I expect numerous people will also do the same, right thing -- to resign in abhorrence that the AMS could be so dense in its science.

Fortunately, I am seeing the change in direction as more colleagues in the atmospheric sciences actually summon up the courage and tell government agencies that they are not signing the IPCC documentation, and they are not putting their name on research that ignores so much scientific evidence showing that natural climate cycles have occurred in the past. And believe me, they are making more difficult decisions than I have to make. I am fortunate that by telling the truth, I have great clients that support my company, Advanced Forecasting Corporation. But some of my colleagues in the field only get paid if they get grant money in, and you can only guess that grant money necessitates that the research is in favor of showing carbon dioxide is a pollutant, carbon dioxide is poisonous, and carbon dioxide is the culprit of any temperature rise.

There is a great commentary by James Delingpole of The Telegraph, titled, "An English class for trolls, professional offence-takers and climate activists" that is brilliantly penned, especially because it comes to the metaphorical conclusion that it might be best to have a Climate Nuremberg, and it pleads that we desperately need change by moving against those that pull the wool over our eyes.

But this change in direction is not only long overdue, it is just the tip of the iceberg. Are you ready for a long sentence? Even though we are now having so many scientists step forward saying that global warming is a big dollop of cow muck, including myself, the multi-decadal intercontinental crusade to compel citizens to recite communication like their ABCs in Kindergarten that increasing amounts of the "pollutant" carbon dioxide will destroy civilization, it is still in the overall plan that governments around the world, trying to become the New World Order, are pressing forward with its plan to tax each individual for his or her carbon footprint, bankrupt local farmers by taxing them on their pig and cow farts, and increasing the probability of an economic disaster much worse than today's shoddy environment.

As I have said before, there is fantastic evidence to show natural cycles on the plane: phases of drought followed by a number of rounds of heavy rains, or hotter periods which rotate to colder periods. It's been going on for centuries, as far back as we can technologically devise a climate record. And for the people with hard hats on out there that work as closet ballerinas (code word for the AGW activists and knuckleheads), the planet is not heating-up, we are in fact cooling down, some areas rapidly so.

Now of course, the Warming Establishment knows all about the current cooling, but they just deny it because they don't want to take their brand new Land Rovers through a drizzle or pick up their iPhones out of the toilet after getting rid of all their methane output, because simply put they just do not have any courage (side-note: actually, instead of 'courage', I was thinking of a five-letter word beginning with 'b', ending with 's' and it has two 'l's' in it and one other letter which is the starting letter for some other very nicely descriptive word of seven letters I had in mind to describe these undernourished cerebral units). These bamboozlers will then try to con you in saying if it is cooling, it's all a part of the Global Warming program. Whatever.

Just look at the "Climate Gate" emails (all public information now) to see how these liars (they are not scientists) tricked, fudged, scammed, fiddled and defrauded the public and their employers (namely, a nice list of liberal departments at universities and government-spun groups, chaired by individuals that are notorious for swindling throughout their careers, if you can call being a con-artist a vocation?).

Let's make something very clear: carbon dioxide is not a pollutant. Carbon dioxide has no color or odor and is a key component of the biosphere's life cycle. And certainly in order to feed the growing population around the world, we need more carbon dioxide to make our agriculture grow better. New studies are showing how more carbon dioxide produces higher yields.

When I start increasing my talking circuit, of course I wish to reach out to all different people of a crowd, but I really want to sit down with our younger-generation scientists that have been inundated with this global-warming crap for the last twenty years, especially the last ten years. Many of them won't speak-up and tell their professors they are wrong for augmenting the deception instead of telling the truth about what is really going on with climate. These younger guys and gals, worldwide, are fearful that they won't get a next paycheck if they don't sign their name to the brown-stained research that gets pumped-out in truck loads, just to get their next government-sponsored check.

In Europe and elsewhere, so-called climate denialists (just another name that the AGWers throw-out to anyone that disagrees with them) have even had death threats. One of my heroes, Dr. Chris de Freitas, the ex-editor of the journal *Climate Research*, published a peer-reviewed critique using all kinds of accurately data and correct conclusions stating the increase in temperatures in the 1990s is not abnormal compared to climate changes over the past thousand years. But certainly, in 2003 when that was printed, at the height of Global Warming, the editor's article was labeled politically incorrect, like this book. Well, you should have seen the pack of

Warming Establishment bloodhounds track him down. They intimidated him no-end and tried desperately to have him removed from his editorial job and fired from his university position. It was absolutely despicable.

I am not kidding when I say the whole AGW crowd is about as deceitful and corrupt as a felon caught doing drug trafficking, perjury, fraud, money laundering, and more. Just follow the money trail, and it stinks to royal hell: see, climate alarmism brings in some sweet dough into the government urine barrels (the ones where they live underground after they detonate a bomb and tell us all living above ground it is okay) which then gets squeezed-out to the academic sector for yes-man verification (although they call it research or collegiate exploration, yeah like feeling up each other in a dark classroom). Then, you guessed it, the government now has a great excuse to raise taxes, and you get swindled the second time around being asked to give the biggest donation possible to AGW-enlisted charitable foundations promising to save the planet. I always keep my most-prized donations for these types of people: first, I tell them my loot is in my backyard, so when they come, I instruct them that they can clean-up my yard of dog poop (5 dogs, figure back-end business a few times a day, hey after a week that's a pretty good endowment; and then hold on, as a special treat, to prove I am not stingy, I tell them they can keep every pound of it as I show them out the gate, dog teeth snarling in the near background). They probably then put it into their carbon models to crank out some more crap, that they can then sprinkle on their granola each morning. Hey, I'm all for recycling!

So, if you start seeing aggressive carbon dioxide controlling or monitoring policies, just make sure to call your government representative and give them a tractor-load of your stuff, fresh on their doormat, because until they get the message that their lies are not going to be accepted any longer, and it is not in the best economic interest of this great country of sovereign states, or any nation for that matter. Let them know that their investment in climate science needs to be overhauled, and instruct them to put scientists in power that don't fiddle with data, tell the truth and share all the information with the People.

The entire climate scam has very little to do with climate. The AGW trojan horse is a political doctrine that revolves around power and a set of laws that could literally take away our freedom, our future and possibly our lives as we know them. These pro-warming people are not interested in the scientific big-picture. They will be defeated because there is an increasingly deafening 'thunder' of broad resistance against the imposed measures. Nothing less than kicking the jackasses out of power will surely help and that is where we come to fame.

In summary, when you look carefully at the facts, connect the dots, and figure that climate (particularly major shifts happening as you read this) controls the landscape, and is a big part of the economic and social outcomes of a country, it is important to know on a personal level that there are things you can do for yourself, your family, and people you genuinely care about and love. Your interest is not only appreciated, but it is absolutely necessary, and I will give you some tips and further insights when we get to the chapter about proactive protection against uncontrollable risks.

CHAPTER 10

GLOBAL WEATHER VOLATILITY, HOTSPOTS & CONTROL OF HUMANITY

Behind Closed Doors: What Can We Expect?

The prediction is rather simple: expect even more severe weather / climate events to occur more frequently than ever before. And the sad truth is that nature is being 'buffeted' by increasing amounts of sprayed or projected unnatural electromagnetic energy, directly originating from the weaponry of the Establishment, including HAARP and other covert operations around the world.

Mother Nature is 'feeling' these increased abnormal doses of electromagnetics at a different vibration beyond its usual receiving frequency, and She is responding in deformed, buckled or distorted ways.

Without a doubt, weather patterns are becoming more unstable. However, in going through reams of data, even though there does not appear to be a higher frequency of atmospheric occurrences of drought, heatwaves, severe floods and other dangers in the last ten years compared to a couple of generations ago, there is hard-core evidence that detrimental climate anomalies are becoming more intense, more forceful and extreme. The list of impacts from volatile meteorological patterns is becoming increasingly longer and more detrimental from the local to global scale as the world's distribution systems and computerized inputs and outputs rely more on each other than ever before. Of course we have a higher population on the planet compared to 40 years ago; and so the mere probability of a large storm hitting a larger population swath with more damage, particularly at the coast, now compared to 1973, is likely going to be higher. That damage is much more likely to be in the form of insurance losses and a downturn in economic activity, not necessarily an increase in deaths, because we usually (but not always) have better evacuation notifications and safer strategies. And in addition, our forecasting modeling abilities have increased the accuracy of adverse weather events compared to the pre-computer satellite-only prediction era.

However, that all said, the worst of any extreme weather and/or planetary threat events are going to Black Swans. And it is not a matter of 'if' but 'when' a large one will occur. For example, as the sun's energy shifts in a new four-pole state, its magnetic energy interactions with Earth is causing more geomagnetic stress which in turn puts greater pressure on volcanoes and tectonic plates, and causes other magnetically-driven intensifications in storms.

Before 1950 when the Industrial Age took-off, there were some horrendous hurricanes, droughts, heatwaves, arctic spells, and floods. Chinese and European records, in particular, can show much evidence of mega-earthquakes. There is paleontological substantiation of megatsunamis that must have been absolutely terrifying with their waves over 100 meters (more than 300 feet) high. When we look back at paleontological evidence, and we calculate solar cycles, we can see similar patterns of planetary intensification related to changes in the sun and also alterations in cosmic rays.

In a nutshell, Earth has always had periods of calm and terror on a planetary disaster scale. Life in general is full of cycles, and so too is our planet's history. Climate has gone through natural phases, sequences and successions (linked to mathematical series) since our planet formed.

In my line of work, I get into more detail in speeches, presentations and other ways to connect to audiences that need more specifications so they can make the right strategic decisions to protect their business interests, assets or just plain get more prepared for what is likely to come. But in time, through the Skyaia® Community online, we will add more and more details.

Here is a description of general upcoming major impact weather / planetary hotspot prediction events for each region of the planet for the next 15 years that represents the 90:10 rule in weather risk dynamics. Please know that **these descriptions represent the top 10% of risk anomalies**. In other words, 90% of the time, weather is tranquil to volatile such that these described major forecast events will either not occur, or not be severe. However, the top 10% worst weather & planetary events in different regions around the world will likely cause 90% of the financial and humanitarian impact. It is these top 10% worst weather events that most people are not prepared for in their lives or businesses.

- **International**
  Weather severities beyond borders with record heat and cold; some years will see global financial impacts exceeding a trillion (with a 'T') dollars; large shifts in fish migrations; Agricultural Protectionism – countries hoarding more of their produce as climates become more notably aberrant; a large increase in climate refugees with large emigration / migrations, especially from cold to warmer climates, with potential climate-related war between China and India; various lands to become uninhabitable like Bangladesh due to super-typhoon floods, others due to radiation contamination like Japan or where nuclear reactors fail due to grid melt-down's, and then others due to a major new plague likely from animal-to-human transmission; skirmishes / wars over access to river rights including river

diversions like the Nile, Colorado Ganges, Danube River and others

- **USA**
  A tsunami hit (from a destabilization of the North Atlantic, including a 'quickening' of planetary risk events hitting the East Coast); new coastal hurricane tracks, rivers break their banks; ruptures (natural gas / magnetically-based) into the New Madrid fault zone from the Gulf of Mexico), drought shifts, and new destructive winds augment

- **Canada, Arctic and Greenland**
  Seasons shift more and more out of balance, icebergs push south, flooding rains increase west and heat pushes northward

- **Central America and Caribbean**
  A region of heightened contrasts: from less trades to stronger hurricanes, and from too dry to too wet; serious volcanic eruptions; migrations northward to USA before the DoD shuts borders against United Nations laws

- **South America and Antarctica**
  A conglomerate of shifting patterns – notably increased warmth / precipitation and storms; smaller countries will be more protected

- **Western Europe and Scandinavia**
  Partial collapse of the Thermohaline Circulation; storms with howling winds, increased floods (and blizzards) and record cold in all seasons push south and east with time; increased volcanic activity over Iceland

- **Eastern Europe**
  Disastrous precipitation spikes and temperature patterns skew out of balance; Russia to become "father" to Eastern Europe to supply energy (and negotiates / barters in supply of energy to other parts of Europe, re-divided after Euro crisis)

- **The Middle East and North Africa**
  Severe weather outbreaks, desert fjords and snowstorms, a new type of heat with so much humidity, and other unusual weather phenomenon

- **Sub-Saharan Africa**
  A continent of severe change: 'flash' storms, new waterways, heating-up the Safari and pushing the Sahara south

- **West and Central Asia**
  Ferocious storms, abnormal temperatures, and springtime rains fail to materialize all take many by surprise

- **Sub-Continent India**
  Large shifts in both the Monsoon (both extremes) and cyclonic storms and life-threatening heatwaves and hailstorms change the way of life

- **Far East Asia**
  Super typhoons, numbing arctic blasts with large snow/ice storms far south, sandstorms (deserts push toward Beijing). Special note on China: increasing famine (from hotter summers and colder winters) and tighter energy and water supplies causes chaos and internal struggles, even threat of civil war; strategic alliance with Russia for energy supplies

- **Southeast Asia**
  A vicious cycle: bizarre temperature changes, drought, blazes and unusual dust/ash-storms due to major volcanic eruption (Indonesia)

- **Oceania**
  Hotter climes, precipitation pattern shifts and humid winds expand bringing some shocking change

- **Islands of the Pacific, Atlantic and Indian Oceans**
  Rising waters west, falling waters east; lower temperatures, less sunshine, and ash in the air turn paradise upside down

However, there is one big difference between today and the rest of history, and this variable could change the expected natural changes listed above. More people are learning about governments and some larger corporations using geo-engineering techniques and weather warfare with increasing frequency and intensity. This technology, mainly electromagnetic in nature, is literally changing our planet's natural vibration, which is not only changing climate but also human consciousness. This machinery is a weapon of destruction that is already having the devastating consequences of causing abrupt weather pattern shifts, such that those in command can now shift the balance of power by bringing on a drought in an enemy nation, thereby causing economic distress by lowering food exports and crippling energy infrastructure that relies on water. This is outright aggression on the graciousness, even the survivability, of our planet! I will get into this in the next chapter, but for now, I will center more on what you can do proactively to protect yourself, loved ones and friends you care about.

Volcanic eruptions in Iceland in 2010 spewed more carbon dioxide, methane and other gases into the earth's atmosphere in a couple of weeks than many years' worth of all similar gases produced by human formation worldwide.

When I talk about planetary change hotspots, I am not just talking about areas that have rising tsunami risk or a higher propensity for more intense vertical or horizontal earthquakes. I am including dynamics that are not often talked about, but that we know happen.

Of course, we have always had earthquakes, tsunamis, volcanoes, meteors and other large planetary dangers. But the scales are tipped toward excessive occurrence of these types of perils. The electromagnetic weaponry that the Establishment uses on our planet causes these planetary events to be more destructive because it has learned how to increase the volatility and intensity of energy flows in the planet's biosphere (on land, in water, and in the skies).

It is imperative that we protect ourselves from truly enormous threats in the future. The Establishment says they have FEMA, and many other different organizations and business continuity plans in place in the event of a planetary disaster, but the truth is they do not. Military documents, both unclassified (that were once classified) and covert, show how governments are causing the enhanced disasters in the first place. Just look into the real reasons of how Fukushima happened. Of course they tell you

it was a large earthquake, and then a tsunami. But that is just a hundredth of the truth as to what happened. The Fukushima catastrophe was so much more than that. It was a military operation, make no doubt when you see the connections.

All extreme planetary events are blamed on Global Warming. And because you and I, as well as swine, poultry and cattle (note aside: we are just barn animals to the Elite), all exhale carbon dioxide, the plan has been for the Elite to literally blame us for the planetary disasters. Their plan is brilliant at a sinister level. For sure, the Establishment are incredibly "gifted" to disguise, because after all, they are master illusionists. But the carbon dioxide "plan" is losing steam, and taking too long. And as more people see through the deception and the illusion, and as more people are disagreeing with authority and not doing as they are told, the Plan of the Elite is soon going to move into the next phase. This next stage is one that brings areas of planetary emergency much faster.

THE JIGSAW PUZZLE OF THE ESTABLISHMENT CAN BE SOLVED

For the Elite, they want to instill terror, and through using their electromagnetic weaponry, they are learning how to achieve their eugenicist goals at a faster rate of return, as sick as that sounds. On our 'Top 10' risk list is a tsunami hitting key First-World cities. This can be achieved by bringing about a triangulated EMP (Electromagnetic Pulse) along different tectonic faults, thereby creating a huge surge in water. Another threat is a directed near-earth object (NEO) collision into a large city. Why do you think NASA is going to spend millions on capturing an asteroid (it's all been in the news)? For any part of the Elite, there is always a so-called "story for the media" that is carefully thought-out, and then there is the covert mission that is in sync with the Establishment's main goals known as different operations under the shell of The Agenda to control the population on the planet and to use those that live through these disasters as energetically-manipulated slaves. Back in the 1800s and prior to that, men, women and children were shackled physically with iron cuffs. Not too far away is the electromagnetic shackling – not just physically but that of the Last Frontier – the mind – that 'computer' which can literally change energy flow.

This is of course the 'race' in the evolution of human be-ings: will it be that enough individuals can break-out of the mold to discover their new-founded abilities with their minds and use the incredible gifts for the positive and to shut-down the nefarious goals of the Elite? Or will the Establishment be the first to 'win' and gain control over the majority of the population? This is yet undecided, but the more people that know about it the better. If the information in this book is not seeded in the right number of hands, then the Elite will win the race, and many of us will become energetically-controlled zombies. Now you know the real meaning behind the Zombie Apocalypse.

So What Climate Changes, Planetary Threats & Other Energetic New Barriers Can We Expect Going Forward?

In other words, as the electromagnetic shell of our planet shifts due to both natural and misused causes, what events will you see happen? Here's a short list of a dozen things that I predict will occur, of which there is no time-line or organization, remembering that imbalances in planetary electromagnetics causes stress on systems (everything from low pressures to engineering projects):

1. Increasing extreme /more intense weather events as well as seasons out-of-place (i.e., snow in June as summer)

2. Ruptured pipelines, causing environmental ruin; a large dam breakage causing an inland water-based tsunami catastrophe

3. Geomagnetic excursion (look up this: the effects of a magnetic field change of the planet would cause

potentially large negative results to computers, and would cause upheaval in the global food / transport systems

4. Major shifts or disappearance of animal / insect / bird migrations; mass die-off's of different creatures, especially those more sensitive or in-tune to energetic inequities

5. Increasing sinkholes, even in urban areas

6. Decreased availability and quality of fresh water

7. A monumental earthquake of 10 – 11 on the Richter Scale, causing the earth's crust to actually be ripped-up

8. Deafening sounds in the atmosphere and lithosphere caused by the warping of attenuated waves of propagated energy breaking through different dimensions

9. Disrupted access to energy supplies due to extensive sea ice and storms

10. Horrendous toxic smells coming from the oceans, as mixtures of gases erupt violently from subterranean channels, causing internal burns, death and inhospitable communities due to repetitive events in similar areas

11. Solar flares causing laser pin-pointed grid meltdowns – some in "Third-World" areas, some in First-World nations

12. Dimensional "cross-over's" causing new realities to be shown (for example, two or more 'stars' in the daytime sky); of course, it will be at times difficult to know whether this is advanced holographic technology or natural-based dimensional warping.

WHAT IS THE ESTABLISHMENT DOING BEHIND CLOSED DOORS?

Of course, the Establishment has their own strategy in case anything they do goes wrong, or if something natural happens unexpectedly. Here's a short-list of ten things (they do not match-up with the previous list) that the Establishment is doing against the goals of peace and prosperity of Humanity:

1. Storage of a massive number of ready meals, the majority of which go to the Establishment first.

2. Enormous amounts of natural medicines, medical supplies and healthcare needs are being taken off the market for their future needs and to lower the overall immunity of the population.

3. Executive Orders (by at least the US President) are rapidly increasing; know that NSPD-51 (National Security and Homeland Security Presidential Directive) is for a real reason … make sure to look this up; the Establishment is doing this for a big purpose.

4. Large seed storage. The Seed Bank / Vault in Northern Europe is just one of many facilities. What do you think they really do in Antarctica? Why do you think the South Pole telescope is built with infrared capability? (Start empowering yourself with answers).

5. Construction of giant subterranean facilities / bunkers including underground advanced water treatment and air purification centers.

6. Shadow governments making their "central operations" away from the coasts.

7. Trillions of unaccounted assets moved to secret locations, many of them underground.

8. Foreign troops permanently on USA soil practicing arrest and detainment techniques, and mass incarceration.

9. A huge and complex multi-dimensional holographic event put on by the Establishment – likely "designed" with aliens – to mimic some religious revelation – and the Vatican steps-in as the earth-based "Savior". For the Establishment, this will be a great show, to increase their power. But for much of the population, unless the word gets out by leaders of the Global Emancipation Citizens United [GLEMCIUN], this event will be very scary, and could seem cataclysmic, putting huge post-traumatic stress on potentially millions. Caution: the movie, "The Hunger Games" will likely take place in some form.

10. Huge increase in elaboration of security to protect assets / places (including stargate portals of which one could be breached) and the elite of the Elite.

Realize that the Establishment also has a number of things that they would do if they fear losing control, and while I don't want to concentrate on these in Skyaia: The Opening®, I will in the future. Of course, many of these are a "replay" of past events. When it comes to control, they check their "Black Book" of what has worked in the past. Don't you know that history is circular? We just keep on playing the same record.

THE KEY TO THE FUTURE

For so long, we never were at the evolutionary point of knowing what was on the other side of our reality: this is the Awakening ... in really finding out our origins, realizing how powerful our minds are, and ... here is the shorter-term more important piece ... if we the People can develop a technology using the SUN and planetary ELECTROMAGNETICS to DESALINATE WATER, then we will not only have extraordinary leverage against the Elite that is trying to imprison us but we the People will unite across borders and see that love not war is the alignment of Universal energy from Source.

The key to this last part is not allowing the Establishment to control this technology. This technology must be given to / developed by the People for the People. Water is the truest BLUE GOLD, more powerful than any energy. But since the energy that will develop the most amazing desalinization process comes from the energy of the sun, and channeled through planetary electromagnetics, we can have so many people come out of poverty and there can be common Abundance so that we do not have the worst wars of the future – the water wars. We can eliminate the water wars by being proactive and seeing the bigger picture of gaining our freedom.

Enough of the never-ending neo-con war-mongering, the piece by piece disintegration of the Constitution and Bill of Rights, and the lies of fighting terrorism manufactured by the Global Banking Mafia. It will not be this way once the People figure-out the plot of the Establishment, and allow the fabrication put upon us.

What The Establishment Has In Its 'Magic' Hat

Here are a list of ten potential insidious plans, some which are broadcast by the championed alternative media but I humbly widen the details, some of which are much more likely than others to try to stop we the People from knowing the other side of our reality:

1. Electromagnetic-weapon-caused commencement of a planetary disaster (like a New Madrid earthquake or

more likely a massive earthquake in a foreign major financial city with a major tectonic fault underneath like Tokyo; or an Atlantic tsunami; or directing a meteorite or small asteroid into a largely-populated area – because don't forget, why do you think NASA has a project on its books now to know how to reel-in an asteroid?); it is imperative to open our eyes to complex Weather Warfare, but of course the more ideal plot will be that which can be very closely blamed on Mother nature, or it will blamed on Global Warming, and the Establishment will tell us how terrible we are for breathing; views of more eugenicists will be broadcast to deepen the Elitist message that there is too much a population on earth

2. Gun confiscation by FEMA Corps or a more advanced 'trickery' – see Project Blue Beam mention below. By the way, a 'civilian army' is very likely to increase, but only when the Establishment stops some of the welfare programs, food stamps and other entitlement programs; then a portion of those people will be 'transformed' (by different types of coercion) into the "New Homeland Army" to "serve" and "protect" and their families will be taken care of very nicely (AND protected – an extra incentive in a society that is increasingly bereft of violence and instability) by Big Brother

3. False flag – they have over 100 different versions in their 'play-book'. Just look up the 'game' of "False Flags" – which can cost a LOT of money.

4. An internet login controlled at the switch: that is, you cannot get onto the World Wide Web unless you type in a government-issued ID (passport, driver's license,

etc.). Of course, there will be an "Underground Internet" accessible without this in the future, like a Black Market Information Channel (BMIC)

5. Martial law – but it won't be called this; you will need special permission to go outside a certain boundary Y if your ID shows your home state as X

6. Aerosolized bioweapons – like a strong avian flu that causes brain damage or renders organs inoperable – or a manipulated-strain Ebola, Smallpox or any number of other pandemics made most likely in the laboratory

7. More than just a bank holiday (the 'normal' but used approach would be to start with a "simple" lock-down and emptying of all "security" boxes): but this time it will be something more elaborate like some kind of Ponzi scheme that wipes-out the loss of trillions from something like retirement accounts all in the name of "protection" of the country; and then of course the Establishment will pedal around some of the 'heroes' that will be brainwashed obviously before going on TV saying that they gave all their retirement account to make you safe. Remember, anything that is "reverse psychology" is a winner in the Book of the Establishment.

8. Look up Project Blue Beam, if you haven't heard about it. Many say this is a conspiracy theory, but in doing a lot of research in connecting many more dots beside this subject, I have come to the conclusion that a shift to this reality is possible now. Here is what I am talking about: there might be a more advanced technological 'fright' into submission by using holographic deception on something that millions believe in (like UFOs or Christ returning to Earth, but it has to be a huge,

absolutely gigantic theme). For example, they could show huge mother ships coming down over multiple cities in the USA, Europe, and China, telling people to come out peacefully and give up all their guns, and they will not be harmed. In other words, it truly will look like some alien movie in real life, right in front of you. The technology DOES exist to turn the entire sky and horizon into a huge plasma channel, and by altering your mental electrical current, you will think you will actually be seeing these mother ships. Millions will fall for it, because in actuality, it might be one of the scariest things you have ever seen in your life, if not the most shocking.

9. Some key figures against the Establishment will be "disappeared", with an educational broadcast of what those people did to threaten The Powers That Be; of course, the Media of Mass Deception (not those corporations and broadcast channels that commit to the People) will color and embellish and outright lie.

10. Thought Weaponization: this could be an "accidental" broadcast of a terrible situation: for example, in the middle of the Super Bowl, a major channel may broadcast the beheading of people in some foreign country. They will purposefully leave it on for about 30 seconds. Then the next day there will be a huge apology by a higher-up. But some people will get all fired-up. The intent of the Establishment is to order the military onto the streets, and there may be a curfew. Again, this is just an example, but it has to be something bizarre and effective that can be "apologized" for, but still incite a portion of the People.

Again, I purposefully copy a small paragraph written a few pages ago: for so long, we never were at the evolutionary point of knowing what was on the other side of our reality: this is the Awakening … in really finding out our origins, realizing how powerful our minds are, and … here is the shorter-term more important piece … if we the People can develop a technology using the SUN and planetary ELECTROMAGNETICS to DESALINATE WATER, then we will not only have extraordinary leverage against the Elite that is trying to imprison us but we the People will unite across borders and see that love not war is the alignment of Universal energy from Source. This is the key to the future.

Chapter 11

Advanced Climate Control: Electromagnetic Technology, Weather Warfare & Radiation

Technological Enhancement Of Planetary Risks

"BREWSTER WAS ABLE TO *HACK* THE *SUBJECT'S BRAIN*, BUT IT TURNS OUT THE BRAIN HAD A *VIRUS*."

These days, compared with any in the past, we have to contend with weather warfare. Declassified military documents show it has been going on for decades. So just imagine the new papers that one could pull out of tyrannical maniacs that explain the very latest machinery.

However, my prediction is that it may not be long now until more ex-military, ex-government or previous employees of large companies become whistleblowers showing the documented proof that there is increasingly sophisticated weather warfare. As a climate risk scientist, I can tell you that so many storms in different 'agenda' areas (USA, Western Europe, Australia, etc.) do not have 100% "natural" signatures to them anymore. That is, storms are a new "rendition" – half natural, half technologically-modified. Through the use of high-powered electromagnetic beams, nano-mirrors, sprays and more, the people in the Elite Forces are purposefully cooling the planet. They are anarchists, simply because this planned cooling is going to create fewer resources necessary for life to prosper. You might say, "well, if that is true, then why in heck would they want more chaos?" THAT is exactly one of the main reasons why you've been 'brought' to this book (and others). It's all about the question of 'control or freedom'? Of course, I admit in empathy to the unsuspecting, it all sounds like a really good sci-fi novel. I wish what I am about to continue to tell you is not true, but there will be countless individuals from all walks of life that back-up what I am saying. And some will say much more.

Just one of the pieces of the climate jigsaw puzzle is the Pacific

Decadal Oscillation [PDO], an approximate 25-year cycle, a magnetic-driven climate anomaly in which not only do certain parts of the Pacific Ocean cool-down or heat-up, but the electromagnetics shift both upstream and downstream. The temperature shift is a well-known fact, but very, very few have entered an understanding of the magnetics. This book's serious talk about magnetics, over and over, in many different examples, both in climate, health and the interaction of the universe with our cells, and more, is just an advancement in understanding, possibly before its time. But I promise you that new discoveries will involve electromagnetics more and more. In 2008, the planet shifted to a 'Cool Phase' of the PDO, and this will last through about 2033, causing increasingly aberrant weather volatility, even into subtropical areas. For temperate zones, expect later than usual spring freezes and floods downstream of oceans (example: USA, Europe), but droughts downstream of continents (example: China); more summer temperature vacillations (heatwaves and unusual cool spells); and, extreme winters in the form of far-penetrating cold into southern areas in the Northern Hemisphere. In the Southern Hemisphere, realize that downstream is the opposite direction, for the most part, to downstream in the Northern Hemisphere because atmospheric patterns flow the opposite way.

Know that there is a going to be a big climate shift from about 2014 through 2029: expect big moisture transport upheavals in China, the USA, Brazil & Australia, incited partially by increasing solar changes (i.e., Cycle 24 into Cycle 25 of the solar sunspot cycle).

THE BIG THREE GAME-CHANGERS OF CLIMATE

There are reams of evidence that support the following statement: the Establishment has purposefully confused and lied to the global populace on the causes of climate change.

When we think of weather, most of the time we think of rain, heat, cold fronts, high pressure airmasses and so forth. When we think of climate (the longer pattern) we think of colder than usual winters, or perhaps seasonal drought or an increasingly windier decade. What is not widely knowledgeable in public climate change are three things – and much of this understanding is kept hidden because they don't want "commoners" like you and me connecting the dots, thinking for ourselves, and realizing we have been deceived.

First, changes in the sun's output is infinitesimally more important in changing the climate of Earth, Mother Gaia, at both the surface and upper levels of the atmosphere, compared to the amount of carbon dioxide produced by humans and all agricultural animals. The sun's output consists of changing wavelengths of light, intensity of solar flares, the shifting speed of the solar wind, the sun's magnetic communication, and a host of other solar variables. I know, we are told the main culprit in climate change is carbon dioxide: well, I repeat it's all garbage. But we will get to all that again. Deforestation, Urban Heat Island Effect and methane do cause some anthropogenic climate change – but again, talk of the solar change impact on climate is squashed by most governments because there is no money for them in blaming the sun. In other words, they can change the amount of sun being received at the surface by using mirrors and other technology, but they cannot directly change the solar output from the sun.

Second, the Milankovitch Theory is incredibly important in understanding climate patterns and is instrumental in showing how our long-term climate patterns occur through a process called orbital forcing (including recession, obliquity, eccentricity, inclination, and so forth). Essentially, there are variations from seasons to thousands of years in how our planet's axis wobbles, which has been a major factor in glacial / interglacial fluctuations. In addition, our high school textbooks deceive us about our journey through space around the sun: we're never traversing the same area of space; we're literally moving in a helix-like shape around the sun: that is, the earth's orbit around the sun is helical, not elliptical or circular.

And third, there is a multi-dimensional, complex communication of electromagnetic energy between not only the inside of our planet to the outer-most layer of the atmosphere, but also between Earth and the sun, as well as Earth and the moon, other planets, and other outer space forces. Our galaxy and this universe is not a vacuum, nor a void, but is a complex area of dielectric physics with new energies that we don't even have the words for at this time. But let me come back to this because it's very important.

THE COMPARTMENTALIZATION OF REAL CLIMATE CHANGE

Here is my researched equation on the factors that go into affecting or impacting global climate change on Earth: solar and cosmic parameters :: 59%, terrestrial and atmospheric :: 29%; anthropogenic :: 9%; and, other :: 3%. These four of course add up to one-hundred percent. This means that the sun (and forces beyond it) has fifty-nine percent influence, on average through a historical time period, in being able to notably alter earth's climate; that is, changes on the sun (and beyond in the cosmos) affect our weather patterns over the long-haul between half and two-thirds of the entire picture.

Solar and cosmic influences is what the anthropogenic global warming (AGW) crowd either don't tell you, they remain ignorant, or they deny it. Obviously, there are times in the past, for example during the Maunder Minimum (approximately 1645 to 1715 A.D.) when there was literally little to no sunspot activity for decades and the solar parameter (to the equation above) then was far higher than the fifty-nine percent. That is when the earth slipped into a rapid cooling and we had a mini Ice Age. There are reams of evidence to support the fact that when solar sunspots go down, the earth cools, and vice-versa.

So let's go into each component a bit deeper, because I am pretty sure you will be interested to hear finally the legitimacy and genuineness of the science being presented here in layperson's terms, that spells it out in detail, and comes at you vibrationally and energetically with accuracy that feels good to you. This is my climate equation:

Solar / Cosmic :: 59% (on average), comprised of:

1. Solar wind flux
2. Sunspot cycles from 11 years to 6,000 years
3. Solar flares and Coronal Mass Ejections (CMEs)
4. Interstellar magnetic / temperature changes (this is an "interstellar communication" deriving mainly of magnetic shifts between the sun and earth, between the galaxy and the sun, and surrounding all celestial spheres)
5. Inter-dimensional energy coming through the sun from other galaxies; yes, the sun does not just 'offer' the earth a vacillating amount of irradiance
6. Cosmic forces (look up 'CERN' and see that they are proving that cosmic rays have long had an effect on climate over eons)

Terrestrial and Atmospheric :: 29% (on average), comprised of:

1. Milankovitch cycles (earth rotation / axis, etc.)
2. Schumann Resonance (our planet's electromagnetic vibrations, proven science with many research stations all over the world monitoring and collecting this data)
3. Volcanoes, wildfires, sandstorms, earthquakes (yes, even tectonic forces can alter weather cycles because as the cracks open from deep within, gases are released and they change the atmospheric ion content and distribution, which then in turns affects the water vapor cycle)
4. Water vapor / atmospheric ion cycles
5. Albedo (reflectivity): polar ice cycles, clouds, etc.
6. Marine current aberrations
7. Methane 'burps'
8. Global salinity shifts (Gulf Stream, etc.)

I realize what you have just read may be very new to you. Much of this is "withheld" from the overwhelming majority of humanity because governments and some of the larger corporations that make the beds of the Illuminati want you to believe that carbon dioxide is the main culprit of climate change … again, so they can tax the heck out of you.

Anthropogenic :: 9% (on average), comprised of:

1. Increasing population most especially in the largest cities worldwide, causing Urban Heat Islands (UHIs)
2. Deforestation

3. Human pollution of truly poisonous gases; not carbon dioxide

4. Radiation (not only Fukushima, but many leaks from nuclear reactors around the world)

5. Technological weaponization changing ionospheric stability, longitudinal wave interference, and ether (aether) stability

It is #5 above – the electromagnetic (EM) and "scalar" (more correctly termed as longitudinal wave) technology – used by the Establishment – **that is at least half of the 9%, and gaining**. In fact, in less than two decades, so-called anthropogenic climate change due to technology manipulations could be as much as 20% of the overall climate equation – more than double of the current 9%! And for placing blame on extreme weather / planetary events, this climate machinery exploitation could be soon to blame for one in five of the disasters since different bigwig countries will use the apparatus for war. That's right – Weather Warfare is beginning already, and before it backfires and/or causes multi-trillion dollar catastrophes, countries with cash or big military might will use hurricanes, earthquakes, tsunamis and all kinds of atmospheric instability techniques as expressions of war. But the key is this: the Establishment HIDES the weapons within the natural events. In other words, these executioners not only embed their weapons into natural events that they know will occur, but also they cause / create the natural storms / earthquakes and other natural disasters too in the first place! And if these anarchists get their way, it is We the People that will be the pawns running for our lives due to super-disasters and an upswing in Black Swans that know no borders.

It amazes me how so many turn a blind eye to countries that commit the crime of river diversification. Water will soon be more precious than gold and oil combined. In fact, my prediction is that there will be water trading on market 'scoreboards' in less than a decade. The toxins (and the Fukushima radiation) that is being dumped into rivers and oceans alike is changing climate patterns, slowly but surely – yet you hardly ever hear about that parameter in so-called anthropogenic climate change. That is because the elite-controlled Mainstream Media do not want you connecting the dots.

By the way, look at deforestation: it's hardly in the news anymore. Forests are disappearing so fast that my children's children will be lucky to be able to visit a beautiful forest. That is very sad. But again, there is not much mention of this anymore, because the Establishment and so many programs usually backed by the elite are focusing on one gas – carbon dioxide.

Realize that governments concentrate on number three, human pollution (from the list on the previous page). But here's the irony: instead of really going after major polluters – the ones that don't give a hoot about putting really bad toxins into the air – the rat-catchers with nets go after who else but you and me, the rodents they say, for breathing out "poisonous" carbon dioxide that is causing hellish increases in our planet's temperature increases. What are we supposed to do, stop breathing, to lower the carbon dioxide amounts? That question may sound strange, but some sick individuals all in pushing eugenics (and Agenda 21) have already said, "Wait a sec, that's not such a bad idea!" And then you have some with too much money and not knowing what to do with it, and go and make some George Guidestones with its first principle saying, "Maintain humanity under 500,000,000 in perpetual balance with nature."

This gets me onto the next one on the list – radiation. See, if some sick Illuminati group wants to kill us off like flies, they very likely have to do it covertly and slowly. And what do you know, here comes Fukushima. Now I might be just called wacky by those that don't get or see the 'big picture' or by those that are trying to set this planet into a perpetual motion of war and hatred. But some people don't like it that I am part of leading the Awakening on the planet. There is coming the day when the ones trying to harm us are getting caught at their own satanic acts. This does not faze me in the least: I know my path, and that is to show the truth, so help me God. This book is getting people on the Path of knowledge. I am combining knowledge in climate, in science and in natural medicine. Can you see where the two fields of climate and natural medicine are now converging? As we are more and more **purposefully** poisoned with toxins and contaminants in our food chain, in our air and in our water, and as the weather patterns move these different poisons, it is affecting our immunity. That is the most important word in health going forward (and I'm prefacing it now so you really truly know).

Your immunity is going to be the one thing you want to protect the most going forward, because it means everything to your life, and it will be the area of your life that will be most bombarded going forward. This is not "fear-porn". The people above the government leaders (and yes, the president of the USA has his "superiors" to report to) do not want you and I leading healthy, happy lives; they want us controlled and in a perpetual state of anarchy, and suffering. You take the time to connect the dots, and if you don't see it yet, take my word for it that this book will awaken something in you subconsciously to delve into your own ways to be able to soon know more.

In continuing with the dramatic releases of radiation from Fukushima Daiichi in Japan, I am more than most appalled. I am revolted and aghast with shock when I see what is happening with this nuclear catastrophe. Do you understand this is nuclear war without the war? Actually, it is a covert war. It is because of the total breakdown in human responsibility, because of the sickening and twisted desires of satanic-loving individuals and groups in the world, the Fukushima calamity has occurred. Mark my words, in review of reams of earthquake activity, there are huge suspicions that this gigantic and wicked feat was caused by some thought processes and actions that are only explained by terror-loving and revengeful be-ings. The Fukushima disaster did not just happen from the result of a "natural" event. Like I said before, the Establishment is clandestinely infiltrating weaponry into natural events, so they are "covered". This tunnel goes down so deep it makes anyone's head spin.

Over years to come, we are very likely going to be horror-struck, and greatly saddened, of course already but moreso in the future, when we see what this radiation stream is doing to our children, our global economy, our environment and our world in general. For governments, environmental agencies and other arrogant talking heads on television to tell me and you all that the radiation coming out of Japan is no more than that of the radiation received from a trans-Atlantic flight or no more than the radioactivity of a banana is absolutely despicable! Who the hell do they think they are? In my atmospheric dispersion modeling work, I watch the radiation circling the Northern Hemisphere, affecting food produce, our health, our immunity and so much more. Immediately downwind of Fukushima is the western United States (including HI and AK), and western Canada: these areas are receiving all kinds of cumulative and increasing radioactive isotopes like cesium, tritium, strontium, uranium, and even plutonium. We are being slowly poisoned in the USA, and less so in Europe, in Russia and other places. The Fukushima mega-tragedy is the biggest crime against humanity ever. In years to come, this will very likely injure, maim and kill more people than the WWII nuclear bombs dropped on Japan. Dozens of times that number of people will suffer greatly with ill health.

Very unfortunately, this may not be the last nuclear catastrophe. We stand, as a civilization, a much higher risk of a nuclear reactor going off-line and going into a melt-down or something similar due to either a solar flare taking the grid down, or a major technical error, or an infiltration by other natural forces, compared to a nuclear war (that is, a country detonating a nuclear bomb on an enemy nation). We have built nuclear reactors in some horrendously stupid locations: on earthquake fault lines, along coastal areas that are open to the risk of a tsunami, and then even worse, we have built cities with larger populations surrounding the nuclear reactors. Some will say that nuclear power is great, but because of the risk of the worst possible disaster happening with uranium or even worse, plutonium, getting out into the atmosphere / environment, I would never ever, if I had the signing authority, allow nuclear

power to go on-line. Again, it's simple math: look at what has happened in Fukushima, Japan, and then tell me in the face that nuclear energy is something we ought to continue to pursue. If you still believe that you are right, then go to Japan and see for yourself what is happening to children (and adults). Go to Chernobyl. Go and see the museums that show the pictures of the WWII nuclear bombs on Nagasaki and Hiroshima. Until you have done that, do not dare to come to me and tell me and the rest of the world that nuclear energy is the best choice we have.

Nuclear energy must go. But then of course we need to expand our minds and think well beyond solar, wave and wind power. What we need is free energy – Tesla energy – that has already been created.

But it has been taken by the commanding financial cabal because they didn't want humanity to be free.

And by the way, here is just a few notes on the last three percent of the climate equation.

Other :: 3% (on average), comprised of:
1. Oceanic trench fissures
2. Methane 'burps'
3. Termites / plankton, miscellaneous.

First, if you take all the termites in the world and you compare their "exhaust fans" of carbon dioxide to human output (not just our exhalation, but also our industrial sources of carbon dioxide), you will find that the termite power, hands-down, wins with many extra zeroes in ten to the X power on the end. Furthermore, do you remember that "new" science that came out a number of years ago that proved that all plants, trees and even plankton produce both oxygen and carbon dioxide? Before this, the high school textbooks wrongly said that plants and trees only give off oxygen.

Second, pig farmers will most readily understand this: methane gas kills, and yet the earth naturally releases tons of it, sometimes in such great quantities that when it rises above from large sub-oceanic trenches or from caves or other surface areas that are usually hotter (i.e., volcanic), we then get some large loss of animal life. You might have heard about a thousand birds suddenly dropping out of the air, or half a million crabs washed-upon beaches with "no apparent correlation" why, so say news tabs. It's usually the natural methane beds pumping away and up, and that gas has to escape; if it doesn't escape, it builds and builds, and then causes an explosion. Sometimes, townships are sickened, and then some say, "We don't know what is the cause." We do not look at the so-called 'beyond' whereas we could be looking into underground methane beds to help correlate some of these examples of morbidity and illness.

Then ocean trench fissures is probably one of the parameters that will most upset the AGW (Anthropogenic Global Warming) crowd because they believe that the pole caps are melting again due to our carbon dioxide levels being too high. And if that's not the exact reason they quote, it's something just as harebrained. These global warming fanatics certainly don't want the average person knowing about what natural processes go on underneath the sea. In polar regions, the majority of ice melting happens from bottom to top, with only a small percentage of it melting from the surface downward. This is because the polar regions have many areas of volcanoes. NASA even admitted this some short time ago, although as you can imagine, the 'punch-line' on the news was very small, and it was then forgotten about a week later. Yes, it's just another fact that is very carefully scratched-out of certain textbooks, and controlled by the AGW agencies that don't want you knowing the truth.

By the way, although the destruction of some coral reefs is natural like from nearby volcanic activity or new fissures that release scalding hot water, sulfuric acid or other concoctions from Mother Nature herself, most of the negative changes to undersea environments are not due to changes in oceanic temperatures associated with the so-called carbon-based 'global warming' movement. Instead, the damage is done by pollution from too much fertilizer, disgraceful mismanagement of waste water, toxic pesticides, leaking oil from corrupt practices at oil companies like the BP disaster in the Gulf of Mexico, radiation (remembering that many hydrogen bombs set-off above ground in atolls in the 1960s are still causing extensive grief including at an energetic level lowering the immunity of the environment there), even massive amounts of Big Pharma residues, and ocean dumping (much of which is not documented, whistle-blown or caught on camera). And the list goes on and on and on. We are consistently lied to on a daily basis, and the brainwashing is such that most people do not know the real truth of the major issues of the world.

POLAR ICE DOES NOT MELT FROM CHANGES IN AIR TEMPERATURE

Volcanic areas under both the Arctic and Antarctica – depending on occasional and cyclical parameters such as solar output, the magnetic output of our iron core planet, the Earth's shifting axis, and other larger 'big picture' factors – become active and cause large cracks to develop under water. Huge amounts of super-heated water, gases and lava rapidly push to the surface, melting the ice. In bigger under-the-sea volcanic activity, and also during larger earthquakes on the bottom of oceanic trenches and ridges that open up large holes, the amount of super-hot material ejected skyward is so immense that it can literally open-up a new 'channel' in the Arctic Ocean or cause a sudden collapse or break-off of a large chunk of an iceberg in Antarctica. Is what I'm saying making logical sense to you? Of course it is, because this is basic science. Yet millions upon millions have been and continue to be hoodwinked, swindled and deceived so badly but so effectively, that they turn on their friends and family and try to force-feed them the same gobbledygook spouting out of the urine-filled troughs of the Environmental Protection Agency.

Coming Back To Multi-Dimensional, Complex Communication Of Electromagnetic Energy

From the outer edges of our galaxy to our sun-earth relationship, it is a web of cosmic electromagnetic (CEM) and plasma communication. This all in turn changes Earth's climate through creation of and nullification of storms, drought, temperature volatility and wind intensity. Of course, throughout Earth's space journey, there have been dimensional rearrangements as electromagnetic and plasma energies have shifted. These incredible processes, well beyond the teachings in the overwhelming number of science textbooks, have indeed affected the physical orbital forcing effects, which moved the landmasses (and oceans with huge tsunamis) on Earth's surface, which then changed the climate of the planet (aka Ice Ages versus the warm periods with wine grapes growing in Scotland). The reshaping of continents and other landmasses did not happen constantly; they happened when Earth (in our galaxy) went through a dimensional modification in space. This is how there has been "instantaneous" huge changes in the past (aka in other dimensions) on Earth resulting in eradication and introduction of different species. In a nutshell, we have a huge puzzle that is all interconnected in a beautiful but intricate way.

> Of course, the world has not been widely educated on cosmic energies (i.e., those from beyond our sun and even from other galaxies) that cause the orbital forcing on Earth that then bring about changes in weather patterns – which indeed explains why they are increasingly volatile and severe when those cosmic energies ramp-up.

Let me return to the 'control or freedom' juxtaposition that we yet find ourselves in again. The Establishment does not want you to think big; they want you to think small, because then they can control you. Today is just like any other point in time: take the 8th century when the Establishment didn't want people reading books to gain knowledge; so what did the controlling forces do? They burned the books to stop people from becoming free. Now in this day and age, in a similar principle, just a different era, a different part of space, it's all about the Establishment telling us that carbon dioxide causes climate change, or in the health arena, they tell us that if you have cancer you must have chemo. It's all lies.

I trust you are getting this: the version you and I got in our so-called 'growing-up' phase was all an invention, a fabrication, a construction of untruths so you would obey, conform and fit in to the rules placed upon you. Many of us are now awakening to the fact that we are controlled. You may not think you are in a prison because you don't see the bars. And of course I'm jumping all over the place here: there are huge connections between climate, cosmic energies, health, and freedom. It is because it is ALL interconnected. It's all a part of the same jigsaw puzzle. It is all a riddle that we continue to solve. That is because we are a part of this enigma. It is all energetics. YOU have to claim your freedom. THAT is the whole point of the meaning of life. Capiche?

THE ESTABLISHMENT'S TOYS & OUR CLIMATE

Less than half a dozen decades ago, the Establishment was regularly 'playing' with nuclear bomb tests. When adversaries showed that radioactivity levels were dangerous in some parts of the world due to these "tests", they stopped. But they began a new set of games, this time not a nuclear competition but a race to create the most powerful electromagnetic weaponry – the EMP (Electro-Magnetic Pulse) bomb. Now of course, we have both challenges: EMP and the radiation of Fukushima (and perhaps God-forbid other nuclear reactors that go offline due to cyber-attacks or solar flares or any other electromagnetic cause). But it goes well beyond this potential EMP attack. There are other weapons and forms of disguised physical manifestations of energy, using incredibly advanced methods of 'free' energy to achieve invisibility, bilocation, so-called "time" travel and more.

Let me tell you something that makes the shivers come up any positive conscious person's back: most people think that a gun, of any strength, can protect them. And to a certain point, they are right. But The Powers That Be (TPTB) consider all guns as 'little toys' compared to their arsenal of incredible electromagnetic capabilities. They believe that guns are for the 'small folks', while their weaponry is far superior.

That is because the Establishment knows that electromagnetic waves, if altered, can not only change but also control your brainwaves and energetic aura (i.e., you can be programmed to be a zombie, or you can be told to kill without any recollection of what you are doing or what you did, or your immunity can be 'shut-down'). So if and when the day comes and the Establishment gets the upper hand in various places around the world, if the People do not Awaken in time, then the ability to control masses electromagnetically will be the method they choose. Again, I know it all sounds too sci-fi and impossible. But once you know the connections between how our brains, hearts, immune system and the Schumann Resonance of our planet works, it is frightening to a bewildering level how the Establishment is doing everything in its power to gain access to every energetic level of our be-ing down to the core. I will repeat

Advanced Climate Control

some of the themes, but I will get into increasing more detail.

Our climate volatility and weather patterns are controlled by a huge number of cog wheels, some much larger than others: the effect of some carbon dioxide gas is so minuscule compared to the guinea-pig testing that the Establishment carries-out with their electromagnetic pulse (EMP) weapons, HAARP, SONAR and other similar technologies that literally smash into, burn, and poke holes in the ionosphere with huge amounts of electricity.

> These weapons also punctuate our electromagnetic auras, our immunity shields. The Establishment is not interested in your true well-being or increasing your health. In fact, the average lifespan -- especially in First World / Westernized countries -- is decreasing (not increasing like you are told) because of two reasons: first, from the huge spectrum and increasing load of toxins put into our bodies AND minds by those individuals, groups and corporations that work with the Establishment and only give a hoot about maximizing control; and second, EMP experimentation with our planet and in particular the climate system, which thereby decreases our resistance to fight disease and ward away pathogens.

Sadly, as you might have guessed, there are some psychopaths and sociopaths in charge of military decisions, laws and financial systems. Some have been coerced, others have been paid-off, and others truly 'love' the control no matter the stakes to others.

Of course, the only way that the planet can come back to less war and more love is by a large number of us Awakening to the realization that the Establishment's principle goal is to control us for the purpose of denying us our given rights to connect to Skyaia®.

That's right: the Establishment does not want us realizing that we have been duped, that we have been lied to for centuries, and it certainly does not want us to know about the ways that they wish to control us much further in the near-term future.

There is a huge parallel and connection between health and climate, technology, the Choice of Humanity – between advancing to peace or continuing with war – and the potential in connecting with someone or another energy in another dimension at a far higher level ever dreamed possible – that is, through your mind, either telepathically or clairvoyantly.

Telepathy and clairvoyance are 'old' gifts that we can all tap into but too many of us have 'lost' the ability to do so due to a multi-lateral 'dumbing-down'. With all these connections, the answer keeps coming back to the power of electromagnetics – and the use of this field for good or evil. That is the future path.

Stepping Back: What We All Need To Do To Make Sense Of It All

I come to you as a private-sector atmospheric scientist with over twenty-five years of climate analysis and prediction experience. I have never been urged, paid or even forced to make any statement or publish any research about climate change against my scruples, ethics, beliefs or knowledge acquired. Because of the insidious control in the huge politics (and dangers: climate scientists in many countries have received death threats if they don't agree with the Establishment-led "Global Warming" and purge of those voices that disagree), I have never published a peer-reviewed article in a climate research journal, but that is all about to change. Since a teenager in the 1980s, I have been particularly fortunate in having traveled to dozens of different countries, and in that journey, I have been able to observe many abnormal weather events – that is, beyond the "normal signature" of a natural event! The time has come for me to voice a very important concern that puts us all in the same boat: the implications of rapidly shifting climate change – not only caused by natural changes but also that which is aligned to environmental terrorism! Moreso, this is all about the huge contradiction between what is really going on with Mother Nature versus the course that the Establishment is leading us down.

Fortunately, for most of the time since 1991 when I graduated from Cornell University with my Bachelor of Science in the Atmospheric Sciences, I have done research on my own accord, and I have connected the theories and other intelligence outside the influence of those that could have forced me not to "look into things" if I had had a corporate job under the auspices of prying eyes. In that, I feel blessed to have been given the opportunity for all these years to have seen and be shown the so-called unconventional truth which is really what drives so much of what really happens on our planet. It's the same with so-called anthropogenic (human-caused) global warming: if I had been working under a governmental entity, or an organization that relied on grants to get its main income, I would have very likely been programmed to believe that carbon dioxide is the chief evil piece that leads to atmospheric heating, and thereby agree with the corrupt EPA and the fraudulent United Nations and its spare wheel in climate change, the IPCC (Inter-Governmental Panel on Climate Change). But, I am fortunate to have my head screwed-on the right number of times and it has been advantageous to have seen the true light in knowing that there have been so many natural changes in the earth's climate, much bigger than at present, without the effect of the so-called human carbon footprint. When you read anthropogenic climate change, we are programmed to now think only of atmospheric pollution, and its main toxin – carbon dioxide. And this fraud is taught from grade school to college-level science! But that is just a drop in the bucket to the REAL anthropogenic climate change. You just wait over the next few years of my career how I expose how the Establishment is changing climate: the technology is pure wickedness, and governments blame it on you and I, and our cattle and other farm animals, breathing and farting 24x7, so they can tax us to increase their revenue streams. All the meanwhile, in the 'background', governments are manipulating the electrical and magnetic "grid" composition of our atmosphere to 'dilate' and contract natural-based energy centers, beams and pulses coming into and going out of the earth that literally are one of the main natural and "intelligent" aspects that balance the huge planet's temperature and winds (for the most part) – all of which is never explained in just about all school textbooks. They simply do not want you knowing about these columns of highly-charged magnetic / infrared and electrical energy.

Outside of the Establishment, the overwhelming majority would sincerely wish to unite together to better protect ourselves against the natural course of climate change and upcoming planetary threats – but sadly, at this time, we have an egotistical, sociopathic, illusionist "New World Order" Establishment setting-up and concocting a deception that is so large such that if one too many egos gets in the way at the top of the Elite, they can literally threaten the survival of our planet. In this absolutely necessary accusation, there is reams of evidence time and time again, that Establishment organizations purposefully changed true climate data with the intent to meet their own political and economic plans. Take "Climate Gate" for example: in the process of this coming to light, the Establishment "sacrificed" a few individuals here and there by embarrassing them and ending their careers, of course after ordering them to fudge the data. But this deceit is so much more than data "re-arrangement". The energy

& economic policy set by the Establishment (claiming global warming) is the opposite way of what is going on naturally (global cooling)!

The Increasing Probability That Our Planet Will Undergo Accelerated Cooling Is Very Real

Our planet is cooling, not just naturally, but also due to the weaponry used (aka infrasonic / frequency ionization weapons). Due to the diabolical use of powerful technology in the wrong hands, we are talking about the use of electromagnetic technology (disguised as Solar Radiation Management) that could not only reflect back too much solar heating (through the use of nano mirrors used in chemtrails, and exploitation of Criegee biradicals, and much more), but also trigger a collapse of our planet's amazingly protective radiation screen – by not only traumatizing, burning and short-circuiting the ionospheric electromagnetic shield – but also radically shifting, rearranging and abusing the magnetic Van Allen belt that surrounds Earth! Their trickery goes to extreme lengths and even the people they once supported to further their goals are later put to shame or put to quiet (in different ways).

In the macrocosm of energetics, every motion and every action has some type of reaction. Earth is rocketing along within our galaxy at 574,585 miles per hour, give or take a few, and in doing so, we're receiving more solar energy every hour than the entire energy needs of human civilization. We are absolutely brainwashed to believe that a billion extra people emitting carbon dioxide and a million cows farting in a pasture is going to make the climate of New York City similar to Jacksonville, Florida in twenty years! Humans are capable of creating, starting, speeding up, and slowing down climate change but the overwhelming majority of this ability is with the weaponry the elite have created, followed by the truly poisonous gases in industrial pollution, followed by deforestation, followed by poor city planning architecture creating an Urban Heat Island. But let me be quite clear on something very important: for our "leaders" to tell us we need to be taxed because of our carbon footprint, they are on way too many Big Pharma drugs and think their number two chute doesn't stink.

All Planetary Forces Are Connected Magneto-Energetically

In another example that planetary energy is connected, the coincidence of hurricanes shortly following quakes is strong too. On infrared (IR) satellite, pre-earthquake IR radiation can build-up to a certain level so that it looks cloudy on the satellite picture, but in reality, the sky is clear to fair. This is sometimes referred to as earthquake weather. You see, the air gets charged with extra ions and it does amazing things: have you ever heard of "earthquake light"? All types of strange phenomena happen, but in reality, what you are seeing is an alteration electromagnetically of the environment. The same thing happens when a charge of magnetic energy comes from the sun and hits the ionosphere to create the beautiful red and green auroras – the Northern and Southern Lights.

And by the way, don't forget that red wood ants know when an earthquake is coming. Ants have chemoreceptors that can detect changes in gas emissions, and they have magnetoreceptors that can detect tiny changes in the Earth's magnetic field.

With regard to whether our planet is warming-up or cooling-down, many have already formed their opinion based upon the media, influential individuals, logic, studying or just plain common sense in poking holes in the crazy claims by governmental agencies that do drug dealing on the side, particularly those liberal leaders that spout their judgment and do shady money transfers into their bank accounts. One illusionist in climate change had a few good years taking us around the back of the building and then feeding us to the dogs.

I'll jog your memory ... start at the lucky seventh letter of the alphabet, his last name has four letters it rhymes with 'bore'.

Because our changing climate has so many wide implications, for the benefit of science and our future path, it is only the right thing to do to tell the true information because as a human race, we are at a critical juncture on making the right decision for the sake of not just future generations but for ourselves today.

Let me be very precise on two important things:
- first, beside a planetary oceanic threat especially in the North Atlantic (due in part to technology in electromagnetics going awry) that could cause dramatic impacts on some major coastal cities, I am overall not predicting massive sea-level rises globally. Just the opposite: I am predicting more sea-level declines. The global sea level rise is just another bogus, sensationalistic, fear-mongering lie from the Establishment. I expect a unique "Coastal Event" to occur that will likely be due to a severe electromagnetic pulse (caused by electromagnetic technology). This severe natural event will be a new form of terror, traced back to the Establishment. Let me be very clear: the rogue elite will cause and then hide behind natural disasters – like a tsunami, or even more complex – a holographic event that will appear very real but will not be. Part of this

trickery obviously involves other dimensions "cloaking" into our 3-D "reality", and was a part of 9/11.

- and second, to reiterate, I am not predicting many large increases in the global temperature. To the contrary: the thermometer read-out of our planet is on the way down into some rapid drops in temperature – due again to two things –solar energy shifts, and the horrific manipulation of our planet's "operating system" of magnetics. The huge wake-up call is not to underestimate the role of technology that is being coerced into natural events.

There are two groups – and I will try to be as non-biased as possible (picture about two inches of buttered sarcasm spread over this piece of toast):

- first, those (including mad-hatter or brainwashed scientists) that love to twist and distort scientific data to show gullible others that humans are causing significant increases in Earth's temperature; the same individuals and groups that push the agenda that human activity / economic output is causing the occurrence of abnormal climate events, based mainly upon anthropogenic production of the "evil" gas carbon dioxide; not forgetting that these individuals / groups only look at climate modeling that does not factor in solar parameters nor water vapor / clouds nor electromagnetics (and certainly never in their wildest hair day the possibility of considering advanced technology that can create storms out of thin air); and that they desperately confuse climate change with being environmentally conscious in the way of limiting one's "carbon footprint",

- and second, those that have carefully studied the reams of evidence of many different kinds that there have always been natural climate cycles, some that clearly show not only on the data sheets but also in historical / societal perspectives that there have been much warmer periods in the past compared with our current climate regime; that not only is carbon dioxide **not** a pollutant but also is good for our environment, economy and agriculture; and incorporate solar cycles, magnetics, and consider logically the impact(s) of sending a billion plus volts of electricity into the ionosphere, and other big-picture ideas to assess the true picture of what is really happening in climate and planetary events.

I humbly thank Divine Spirit that I have applied myself in life, and that I have soul and courage to firmly plant my highest confidence in the second group. But wait, before I have some hot-blooded fools trying to scream bloody murder at me and grouping together other easy-to-fleece individuals all then screaming 'racist', 'unpatriotic American', 'oil-pusher' and other sometimes fantastically-creative names at me, or give me worse, always of course acting completely out of emotional toxicity caused by a thorough brainwashing by some mouse turd-riddled Establishment, let me be very specific, because there is only the need to say this once: I am not a 'climate-denialist', I care a lot about our environment, and I agree that humans are causing some climate change.

Wait, what was that last bit? That's right: humans are causing some climate change. Now come on, Simon, you just contradicted yourself. No, re-read. I said that carbon dioxide is not an evil gas, carbon dioxide is not a pollutant, and that carbon dioxide is not heating-up our planet. I said that there are much more effective ways to cause climate change: the ones doing it know it all too well. Go back to the scratch-book and let's focus on the truly noxious fumes, the chemtrail spraying (aka Solar Radiation Management – nano-sized mirrors that reflect back sunlight that will really cause runaway cooling in suburban and rural areas), and the other electromagnetic "priming" or pumping-up of a storm (or the broadening of a drought by 'sucking-out' the positive ions from the air that cause the water cohesion in the first place). Oh yes, the rogue elite know what they are doing. And if you are in doubt, take yourself down the deep set of tunnels that I dug through to connect the dots and see the military, NASA and CIA documents that fuse together very hard evidence that so many governments are meddling into something called "Environmental Terrorism". Yes, I know – it's terrifying. Pull yourself together and realize that it is not me lying to you, it is your government that is lying to you. Many don't want to know, and I can't say I blame you. It's simple to understand that many don't want to leave the comfort zone of their latte and tweeting on a tablet while waiting for a pedicure.

What They Tell Us We Must Do Is Completely Different To What They Do

Let's do a quick recap: it's not you or me causing an increasing amount of the climate change. It's some really malicious people. They know that there are much faster ways and much more effective ways to cause climate change (and for the elite, it goes well beyond that as the ultimate 'mission'), without waiting decades for really poisonous gases, not carbon dioxide, to infect the earth and cause a marginal increase and even a negative feedback loop cycle of a decrease in global temperatures (depending on the factory-polluting gas).

These evil-doers know that in order to change Earth's climate, they have to 'play' with (a.k.a. alter, modify, fiddle with, amend, regulate and control) the "Top Guns" of natural climate change: the sun's output (and/or the amount our planet receives, hint hint), and electromagnetics of the magnetosphere and ionosphere.

We don't need to ask the sun to change its heat output, because the sun already does this on a natural, cyclical basis. In fact, there are many different-year cycles of the sun, including the sunspot cycle of 11 years, the Hale cycle of 22 years (when the sun changes its magnetic field), the Gleissberg cycle of 70-100 years (87 year mean), the Suess cycle of 210 years, the Hallstatt cycle of 2,300 years and a 6,000-year cycle and more. These cycles all have tremendous influence on Earth's climate cycles as heat and magnetics shift on the sun.

So guess what "invention" these panicked agencies come up with to decrease the amount of solar energy received by our planet? You got it, they said, 'Dude, let's reflect the sun back to cool down our global warming!' And so now you have secret programs, which aren't too secret anymore, that are cleverly-designed nano-size (super tiny) particles that reflect back light. Of course, there are trillions of them, spewed out into the atmosphere, at different levels (by aircraft in the weather-making layers, and even by the International Space Station 'thrown' down from above at a constant rate). Yes, you're right, it gets 'wild'.

And then you have the ionospheric electromagnetic controlling technology. The government has done a lot of dark-room, behind-the-hill research on Earth's beautiful electromagnetics, a vibration called the Schumann Resonance. Look it all up, and connect the dots. The military has openly admitted that it's using weather warfare. This is no more a game of science fiction, this is really happening. Well, these behind-the-scene top-guns, you know the good ole' boys who hide behind mirrors and had to ask mommy at 18 years old if they had permission to take a leak, also found out that the Schumann Resonance not only affects our planetary climate pattern, but also influences the mental and emotional states of human beings.

Boy, they were really toasting the champagne when they had this gig all sussed-out. They kicked-back their feet, and said, "We can control the climate over that competitor of ours AND we can control those multi-billion pee-on's (less than a billion of the mat-wipes once we get done with wreaking havoc with their immune systems, interfering with their fertility cycles, and controlling their mental actions), and then, we can tax a brick-load on their carbon dioxide output. Just fricking brilliant, Elliot!" Do you see this huge picture they are crafting? Technology exists that can change the frequency of the planet. But why is that important? Ahhh, this is where it gets interesting.

STRATEGIC ELECTROMAGNETIC CONTROL IS THEIR GAME

So here comes HAARP (part of the Strategic Defense Initiative), and SONAR, and other ways to change the electromagnetics and acoustics of our planet. Just read Zbigniew Brzezinski's book, "Between Two Ages" to read about unconventional weapons using radio and magnetic frequencies, under the premises of ENMOD (Environmental Modification). Ultimately, the military implications of these projects is very disturbing. Projects like this are "sold" to the public as some type of strategic initiative like a space shield (against incoming asteroids), but in reality, they are modifying the world's electromagnetic field. They realized that our planet is the most beautiful instrument that they have ever seen. And what better thing, they thought, could they do than pluck the strings so hard that they mess things up but then they'll blame the bad 'music' on those breathing the carbon dioxide? Their whole gig is to make the pee-on's pay-up, so the elite bankers get tons of new revenue to grow government into a superpower all in and of itself, and they will have control of everything. So they think.

Not so fast.

Those that think they are too clever to get away with it are all mistaken. The planetary awakening is happening at a frenetic rate now, and the evil leaders trying to put us into pig pens are getting worried that they cannot carry out their exploitation operation and manipulation sequence (what I call EOMS) in time. The tide is changing, and more are waking-up. When you realize what is really going on, it's as if some nasty-smelling toxic odors are coming into your lungs. And we see what is truly going on: even if there is Fukushima radiation increasing on Geiger counters in the United States of America, many see how trivial this is to much of Mainstream Media. It is time for Community Leaders of the Awakening of Humanity Against Tyrants (AHAT) to stop the madness.

See, the huge squabble on planetary warming versus cooling dates back to the 1970s when TIME magazine had a cover story on the possibility that our planet was entering a new Ice Age because so many countries had become noticeably colder, some with huge blizzards compared to previous decades' observational measurements, energy demand (despite population increases) and general experiences.

Granted, at any given time, in the overwhelming majority of circumstances, there are regions on the planet that are cooling and there are other parcels or pockets that are warming. The natural system does an excellent job of balancing the cold and heat, but without a doubt, there are times when either below normal or above normal can become dominant. I always like to think of the planetary temperature balance as a see-saw or a tug-of-war. If one side clearly gets the advantage, it can take a while before the other side gets its time to shine.

Even proponents of Anthropogenic Global Warming (AGW) cannot deny that grapes were grown plentifully in England in parts of the Middle Ages because it was so much warmer than compared to now. And no, sorry AGW'ers, it wasn't just a shift in the Gulf Stream back then ... places all over the world were seeing temperatures much warmer than today.

In the world of climate science, it is incredibly unfortunate for all Earth citizens that there has been so much dishonesty, bribery and outright fraud in different research programs being funding for the advancement of a political agenda. In addition, there has been so much "fiddling" including deception and falsification with atmospheric and oceanic data collected from around the world. Climate Gate was the largest uncovered scam, but there is much more trickery, swindling and cheating going on with meteorological numbers at all levels from Establishment to university level (that has not yet broadly come to the surface by Mainstream Media).

In actuality, the IPCC (Intergovernmental Panel on Climate Change) is a complete joke at best, a corrupt agency of factual distortion in the realm of science, and a criminal group of insiders that play to the whims of the Illuminati at worst. In a decade from now, perhaps far sooner, it is my prediction that the IPCC will be put to rest, with a tombstone that reads, "DELINQUENTS. Misled Humanity for decades". The principles of this group will go to the grave with the main felons never admitting their outrageous crimes that have literally helped to bankrupt a part of the global economy because economic decisions were made which ultimately relied on the myths and transgressions that were parceled-out of this corrupt institutional mental asylum of egotistical gluttony.

Fortunately, there is hope in this huge data scandal, that has without any doubt infected even some larger higher-ranking American institutions of governmental science, but there is likely not going to be any reversal in the current lunacy until a strike-back of some major kind, the type when people are so fed-up with being taxed to the hilt in the first place, and then they learn all their IRS-commanded taxes for their carbon dioxide footprint have been just a bunch of lies. There is no doubt in my mind that there will soon come a time when we will need to embark upon a massive project to re-scrub and essentially clean-up all fudged climate data points. But at current time, and for the foreseeable future, unless something miraculous occurs, like having a new president of the United Socialist States of Amerika say that she or he is turning the clock back to apologize for all the wrongdoing in making the field of atmospheric science into a complete travesty, then the next decade ahead will be dark, increasingly dark on the climate scene. Metaphorically, there will be nimbostratus clouds often producing vivid displays of lightning, high winds of record-force, and a reduction of the solar angle across the whole earth giving an eerie glow to outdoor lighting similar to the day-length in Prudhoe Bay, Alaska in late October. The bottom line is this: the world of weather is being hijacked. The Establishment is using weaponry to exploit natural occurrences, and the government is using front groups to manipulate climate data to their favor to advance an agenda. So much needs to be told, and we will get into this, but first, let me get into what the real climate equation is all about.

The basic premise is we need more thinkers and whistleblowers. Instead of the government wasting trillions of dollars on the Military Industrial Complex, making weapons to exterminate and damage, we need to instead put our financial competence into thinking conciliatory solutions! For the future, instead of the terrible woes that come with nuclear energy, we could come up with harnessing energy using the power of magnetics, of levitation, of longitudinal wave (scalar) energy, of zero-point energy, of geothermal (although there are niches where this has really delighted), and of course the less-well-known of inter-dimensional energy (aka how the sun harnesses its power in the first place).

Regarding of energy sources, you almost never hear about geothermal warming and the relationship to undersea volcanoes, even though we now know much more about geothermal energy and the ocean's thermo graphic imagery showing heat 'cells' by special satellites and other equipment. Or what about anti-matter (which is already being used in PET scans)? How about sonoluminescence (the same energy used in the creation of and powering of the stars)? How about Thermal Conversion (or TCP)? How about OTEC (Ocean Thermal Energy Conversion)? And what about technology to make coal burn cleaner? There is so much in Tesla energy, many books have been written about it – and then banned. Why!? In summary, "they" say there isn't a way, but how do we truly know? Of course, look at so much of the solar magnificence that is going to waste in the USA Desert Southwest and other very sunny climates (beside the few solar panels out there 'grabbing' a mere iota of it). Or how about all the surplus, untapped wind power stretching from North Dakota to Texas and other windy areas? What about the incredible strength of the Gulf Stream right off the SE coast of the United States? The private sector is really churning-out some ideas -- and yes, I greatly applaud all the ideas of inventors, investors, and scientists that are really thinking. It's all "out there", we just have idiotic leadership (with the exception of some countries) that thwart these possibilities because they get lobbied by some loony group that says we ought to pay more attention to keeping huge underwater turbines out of our waters because they will kill dolphins (when this excuse is so lame because we can easily protect wildlife) -- the same massive blades that could use the extreme power of the Gulf Stream to power-up industry! Let's go back to those dolphins: part of any new technology would require it to be completely cognizant of the environment with full respect and love of all creatures so that they do not get hurt.

Realistic? You bet it is. Private automobile companies are making cars in which the only emission is water; but sadly, the government is choking-up the distribution outside the areas where the solar power is plentiful enough to make free hydrogen so that hydrogen stations can be constructed with a good return-on-investment. Time and time again, the best of technology and the most brilliant of ideas that COULD steer humanity in a much different and positive direction are 'taken' by a bunch of sub-human entities that are none other than malicious, criminal and pathetic hijackers. And this has been happening for centuries.

Some of the blame is with us: we, the People, have our priorities in the wrong place. Here we are, constantly fighting about this, that and the other. Too much of the human population praise leaders who try to dominate other nations and take away their resources. If we just minded our own business, and got so many more teams together to t-h-i-n-k, and re-learn to dream and figure-out how to protect ourselves from radiation dangers in the air and water and food (and stop those from purposefully putting the dangers there in the first place), then we'd be on such a better track. If so many governments did not restrict the news, then we could really accelerate our civilization to new heights. I talk more about this in Volume

2 where I ask teachers to stop teaching about war battles, and instead start teaching our children about ways to be more peaceful. Please, for God's sake, let's stop the madness and wake the heck up. You better believe I am passionate. I am a Light Warrior – defined as someone who is seeking harmony and abundance for humanity. Because frankly, what we are doing as a civilization at this time, is not working: war does not work, it just breeds more hate and then more war follows. And certainly, coming back to climate, if so many of our so-called elected leaders and officials in a position of command and jurisdiction, could just tell us the truth about what is really happening on our planet, that would be a start.

Most would really like to know why governments feel that pumping a few billion volts of electricity into our ionosphere is their right. It is not. These officials know too damn well that their "experiments" are so-called "advanced" weapons of control. Just look up HAARP to begin your empowering journey of new knowledge. There are already top-secret operations that are well above the power of HAARP because once upon a time, HAARP in Alaska used to be top-secret before it was uncovered. Now of course, officials up there and beyond tell news agencies and individuals that nothing sinister is going on with their array of towers emitting gigantic 'shockwaves' into the upper portions of our planet, which destroy our protective layer, which ripple down causing earthquakes and climate disasters. I mean, where is our news reporting going? What happened to getting at the truth? Are we so afraid now that we can't step on toes to get at answers, truthful responses? Good grief. It's sad. And now there is going to be a lot of people buying Geiger counters, so if you want something that could save your life, think about monitoring radiation.

There is so much to talk about: I think it would be a good idea for me to have my own talk show (TV or radio) in the near future. I intent a group of people to please make it happen. I am sure there will be at least a few groups out there that will say, "Bring it on, we're ready for you!" It might be called Simon Says Radio, or Skyaia® TV, and we'll get so many on the right path of thinking and peace to help get the USA (and other countries) turned-around again, all after old-fashioned principles and values.

China Is The One Of The Larger Loosening Lugnuts On The Climate Wheel Of Humanity

Expect China to see a multi-year drought. China is no dummy, they know that the drought is coming, but of course they don't want to cause an outright panic so they don't mention much.

First of all, citizens of a country would much rather not only want to have, but need to have, the truth of what is really going on climate-wise, instead of brushing the reality and legitimacy of real science under the carpet. So, perhaps at some point soon, we the People should show the governments how to tell its citizens the truth by returning the role of government under the power of the People. It is only when the People know they are not getting the truth does an outright panic develop.

So what is China doing, knowing that they simply do not have and will not have enough water to keep its population gathering and working peacefully in years to come, and have its economic engine humming along in its goal to reach a superpower status. Oh yes, climate aberrations and interruptions (namely of lack of water) are coming to China, and it could very well stop the Chinese from becoming a superpower. The overwhelming number of investment reports do not talk of this climate challenge with regard to China.

All major civilizations in history have succumb to defeat when there has been too much drought, especially when famines have hit consistently. Of course, in the global village concept of distribution, it is highly unlikely that China would ever come to the poverty level of any of a list of the most drought-stricken countries in the world, simply because it has a lot of cash and is amassing resources at a record pace. But what I am saying is that China might have to get used to reversing its status on the global chess board of currently being able to purchase X water rights in the United Kingdom, Y mineral rights in Angola, and Z ethanol rights in Brazil, and so forth.

In other words, if China does not get enough water in future years to keep its coal, nuclear and agricultural industries singing at an A-flat pitch, the most likely scenario is that China will be getting a proverbial economic and socio-political fever of dire proportions. The Chinese government knows this – and they know their biggest threat is a social revolution. Only the smartest are connecting the factor of climate change into their logistical analyses, and strategically emphasizing the future costs of doing business in China IF the swimming pool dries up and its once moist walls turn to a scraping of dust.

So what has China done to try to offset this drought risk? Just like they ran over people in Tiananmen Square, the Chinese leadership invaded Tibet, a sovereign country, led by His Holiness the Dalai Lama (who must reside in India otherwise the Chinese would imprison him). By the way, most maps you can buy today, especially those printed in China, do not show the word 'Tibet' anymore. The objective of China back in 2008 (often known as the 'Tibetan 2008 Unrest') was not to stop a few Buddhist lamas and monks from crying-out against the Chinese demanding that Tibetans merge into the "Motherland". Oh no, it was much more sinister than this.

The Chinese knew that the Tibetan Plateau holds the largest amount of fresh water in the world in one location, and it knows that if it builds pipelines and train tracks from Tibet eastward into major rivers of China, it can then secure more water for its authoritarian and tyrannical needs.

China also knows that it can try to divert international rivers so that more water flows into China than the neighboring country. China has diverted the Mekong River (and others) in the past. China tried more recently to do the same with the Brahmaputra River that flowed into India, supplying the Indians with some additional water in their dry season. But India was clever: they caught the Chinese with satellite technology showing the change of river flow. But when push comes to shove, what if the Chinese threaten a country, or do some kind of narcissistic deal where they offer other resources, say output based upon the water given (i.e., the Chinese give more electricity to India, after the additional water from the Brahmaputra River goes through hydroelectric turbines on Chinese territory)? The Chinese would try to appear that they are doing a so-called humanitarian thing, sort of like what some Administration said was happening when they invaded a North African country in recent years, both of which are complete lies.

CHAPTER 12

LOWERING YOUR IMMUNITY & CONTROLLING OUR MINDS THROUGH WEAPONRY WE CANNOT SEE

The Eugenic Ploys Against The Human Awakening

Make no mistake about it, much of the technology, especially the darker side used for weaponry and control of the human mind, that has been proven to cause interferences in electromagnetic fields (EMF's), is increasingly more dangerous, as its uses become more widespread. Their negative interactions with both our planet's electromagnetic fields and the human energy field are grossly underestimated to humanity's detriment. However, there is hope.

There is probably not going to be any decrease in technological EMFs in the immediate future, unless there is a very significant solar flare in the near future that could take-out large parts of the technology that produce EMFs. In fact, there is very likely going to be an increase in the EMFs that bombard an average person on an average day. Therefore, the best way for personal advancement is first to understand what happens and then second to protect yourself. This strategy is similar to … if you are a non-smoker … to avoid places where cigarette smoke is most likely to occur, but also to go through a detoxification process of any type to increase the probability that more toxins are in fact being eradicated from your system.

Look how smoking in the 1960's went from medical doctors as members of the American Medical Association (AMA) vociferously recommended people to smoke cigarettes to new research in the last few years that now shows the great deal of harm cigarette smoke does to non-smokers with them breathing in smoke around smokers. A similar understanding of technological EMFs and their negativities will become well-understood, although realistically, because changes are happening faster and faster, the shift will probably happen more quickly.

First, it is best for us all to understand how our natural defenses work. Every day, most of us are bombarded by EMF's that are harmful because they "invisibly" break-down our auric shield which is much responsible for our greater immune system. I say 'greater' because in essence the human system has at least two immune systems – an external one and an internal one. The internal immune system is the one that allopathic medicine has studied for decades. The external one is the one that Eastern and alternative medicine has studied. The human system is 'designed' even more cleverly than we can ever begin to fully cherish. Just like a bank has at least two sets of barriers set-up to stop potential robbers to get into its most important safe, the human system has at least two hurdles to stop potential pathogens to get to its respiratory region, lymphatic nodes or other important areas.

There is no bias in what I am about to say: the external immune system, the electromagnetic shell that surrounds almost every human being is far more important. In fact, the Pareto Rule comes to mind here: the external gate stops at least eighty percent of the potential intruders from entering our body. While the external obstacle concentrates on numbers, the internal barrier gives attention to the more intense invaders, that is, the ones that are perhaps more persistent, more intelligent and more powerful.

Of course, if a criminal gets through all systems of a bank … if s/he cuts the lock on the outdoor building gate, then has a computer to crack the alarm system code for auto door open, and figures out all the different ways to break into the inside safe … then the system fails and the thief gets the gold bars. The same is true with the human body. If a flu strain is particularly strong, and one's external energetic field is temporarily going through a 'software patch' or is just 'down for the count' due perhaps to multiple previous attempts to knock it down, then that next virus could indeed have a higher probability of getting through, weakening or destabilizing the body in various ways, and if really strong enough, and the internal immune system is also on marginal power, then the person may die.

There is no conspiracy theory in the 'hidden' agenda of the increasing use of electromagnetic technology to literally break us down (immunologically) and dumb us down. The breaking down is hitting our immune system repetitively and cumulatively until we become sick more often (or more sick) and we then turn to more drugs, chemicals and pills that contain toxic materials that further debilitate us. You can imagine what this does to infants or children that start on Big Pharma drugs, like Ritalin, where the overwhelming majority of them are put on this lunatic track by crazed psychologists, dead-beat school principals, and power-hungry officials at Child Protection Agency (CPA) and other rotten-egg corrupt places who force or convince parents that their kids are out-of-control when really they are only running around having fun, just like kids did one, two, five generations ago without any reason to believe they were acting 'strange'.

Look At All The Things That Have Changed To Hurt Us

The things that have changed in this generation with respect to kids are as follows:

1. family values have taken a plunge, and family unit cohesiveness has gone down;

2. too many kids are being raised by their television sets and video games, many programs and games of which

are violent; in addition, Big Brother is adding in the mnemonic circles – the Mind Control programming – and if you know nothing about this – look it up to go down a dark tunnel indeed;

3. let us make no mistake about it – Big Pharma is a silent weapon against humanity. An extraordinary number of children and teenagers are on Big Pharma psychotropic drugs; this is the real main reason for such a huge escalation in the violence of young people – that is, where you find the high prevalence of Big Pharma dominance in a society, such as the United States of America, the amount of gun-related and other types of violence is going to be extreme; just do the research on the overwhelming number of extreme crimes (mass shootings, etc.) and you will find that all the crazies that perpetrated the crime were either taking massive amounts of legal drugs from pharmaceutical companies or they were mind-controlled (we'll get to this), or both;

4. many parents put more "love" into their acquired material things than into the brains and bodies of their children, not stopping to think about the general ill care of most daycare centers that concentrate on profit rather than love – although as much of the world slips into an economic depression – this trend of parents seeing their priorities is ironically shifting back, although potentially more is forced than realized;

5. toxins in the average body have rapidly increased: average children, unless they come from homes that stress an organic and alternative health lifestyle, are hyper-toxic – full of GMO foodstuffs, vaccination poisons like formaldehyde, alum and bi-products of

aborted animal RNA (even if doctors are saying that the mercury is out), soft drinks leading to a rapid rise in diabetes, fluoride in water causing organ degradation, and the list goes on and on;

6. a huge increase in 'dosage' to strong EMF's, causing a surge in brain cancers from cellular phones in particular, an increase in personality disorders, anger and irrational behavior from spending too much time on the Internet, on virtual reality or solitary / competitive video war games.

7. and make no mistake, those so-called "smart" meters that the local utilities are putting in your homes are NOT about saving energy, they are about sending out a specific electromagnetic frequency (when "requested" by authorities or higher-up's) to change YOUR behavior. Yes, I know, it all sounds too sci-fi. But it is all so real and too real at that. There was no "opt-out" with this smart-meter installation plan across America. If you refuse, police will accompany the utility worker in its installation. The electromagnetic pollution from these "smart" meters breaks-down one's immunity, and interrupts with your REM sleep, increasing the probability for sickness (and I know this is going to sound like a long-shot, but you will find out that this is exactly what the "System" wants so you can be more governed). Long-term, these "smart" meters can cause more serious dis-ease. This is where it is important to buy a device that cancels-out the negative frequencies. Of course, those trying to control us as a herd of animals, do not want an increasing number moving "off the grid". Self-sufficiency is not only frowned-upon by the System, it will not be tolerated in the future.

It never ceases to amaze me how some blame more bizarre behavior and an increasing list of irrational states of mind and the subsequent actions of people below the age of twenty-one years old on easier access to guns and other weapons. This excuse is complete hogwash. It goes back to the erroneous old argument that guns kill. All acts of violence need a catalyst and an action – a person pulling the trigger or a software program that counts down the time until the bomb explodes.

Just look at the behavior of "flash mobs" of recent times causing curfews to be set in major cities in different countries. It does not take an Einstein to recognize that this "new" episode of crime is due to multiple reasons, many from the list above. But so-called "officials" and even parents don't want to hear that blame could be tracked back to their ineptitude, and certainly Establishment is turning a blind eye by steam-rolling through toxins into our food chain and public water systems without even seeing red flashing lights in front of them.

Let's face it: the System world-over is breaking-down. Now granted, every generation has faced crises in society, but today, the challenge to health from a more intense and more frequent set of negative energies has never been higher. In addition, if we go back to the electromagnetic fields (EMF's), our climate system has never had such a large challenge presented to its normalized set of parameters than today. Let me very blunt: the technology in the realm of electromagnetic and deviant actions that the Establishment and powerful corporations that get into bed with each other take are having a large effect on destabilizing the normalcy of weather patterns and climate trends.

Now sure, there have been different climate patterns since day one, millions and even billions of years ago. But it is a total sham for the Establishment to come out and lie when they announce that it is carbon dioxide that is changing our planet's climate system. This is a total sham. What you are not told is that the military, large corporations, boutique research companies in physics and other scientific areas with ties to Establishment officials, as well as well-known public figures even inclusive of well-known actors / actresses are all in on the sting of making you think that your carbon dioxide output is dangerous. They tell you to cut down your "carbon footprint" while behind the scenes a billion volts of electricity is fired-up into the ionosphere, causing a huge generation of heat and a destabilization of atmospheric pressure systems. Oh yes, this time you are hearing it from a climate scientist: one that does not want to sit back and sit merry watching 'fake' clouds appear across the sky, does not want to be fed a load of horse crap for breakfast and run along in the park telling everyone how the Establishment is doing its best to stop evil companies from increasing their carbon footprint.

There is a host of weather warfare technology being tested all over the world. The destructive force of this weaponry disgusts me to the end degree. And this is no contrarian theory. Do the research, connect the dots, and discover the truth for yourself.

Make no mistake about it: the Establishment, some corporations, and some individual sponsors are gleefully masturbating like insane chimpanzees over their new toy of electromagnetic weaponry.

Technology To Alter The Frequencies Of Your Mind Already Exists

And if you have a very sick and twisted mind bent on conquering the world, just like a modern-day Julius Caesar, what greater idea could there possibly be than to dump a ton of money and research into technology that could cause a huge flood, direct a hurricane into an enemy city, enhance a drought over a large agricultural area, or even catalyze a large earthquake over a major city, and here is the best part from the psychopath's thinking, there is not a trace of evidence or a breadcrumb path of blame for the magnificent work that damages, kills and otherwise upsets the lives of thousands if not millions of lives.

It is a real challenge not to foam at the teeth when you know the truth of actions taken by such perverted souls.

Just to show you more of their sick fun, because I know those responsible for such electromagnetic-induced mayhem are getting their biggest woodies watching me put myself in a hole whereby so many liberal-minded idiots can make fun of me, let's go further.

Those that are penetrating the full abilities of technological EMF's have gleefully found that they can change the natural EMF's frequency. Now, it is scientifically proven based upon the connection between Schumann resonances and the field of sleep science that the tipping point of being able to control a region's EMF frequency is within the capabilities of current technology but it is not enhanced enough to be able to successfully regulate at will the EMF to a setting of their choice. That is, modifications to the technology are needed before these messed-up individuals acquire the ability to change your city's EMF.

So, when your local EMF can be changed, what does that mean? That is where the big Pandora's Box is opened. It will do at least the following two things and probably much more:

1. the Establishment or controller of the system will be able to alter the frequencies of your mind. You see

where I'm going with this, don't you?! Let's say I was at war with City XYZ, and I had a good cup of coffee and thought up a plan of changing the frequency of the average REM (Rapid Eye Movement) of City XYZ's population, I could effectively radically alter their sleep patterns. We all know what happens when someone goes without sleep for one day, two days, and then, well, let's just call it that famous ole' Big Pharma "side effect" called death. Oh wait, but that technique is just too quick; no, too many people will catch on, they have to do it more cleverly than that. So how about just changing the frequency of our minds to activate a tripling of our cerebral centers that regulate anger. Then we could have the citizens turn more violent, crime would instantly go up and everyone would be in arms. Call it a mini civil war. Then the government could call for military checkpoints, just like they are experimenting even now in some States, a curfew in certain cities, and more mechanisms of control. In the meantime, depending on how sick my creativity was if I were one of these Establishment Commanding Officers, I could sit back and let it go on for a week all the while monitoring it by high-resolution spy satellites or drones. It could become chaotic so I'd have to watch that my Establishment buddies didn't get hurt; oh wait, I'd send them a memorandum beforehand advising them to get out of Dodge before I pull the 'switch' (hopefully they check their alerting e-mail and aren't taking that fishing trip to Lake Mellow, in the outskirts of town).

2. weather would become so volatile that perhaps depending on the modulation of the frequency of the

EMF, I could induce a huge rainstorm and say have thirty inches (762 mm) of rainfall in a 24-hour period, when the total annual rainfall may only be twenty inches (508 mm). This may cause destruction of twenty-percent of the buildings, totally jeopardize energy power sources and water purification centers, and, well, you get the picture.

I can only come up with two things for now because unfortunately my training in being sick and twisted is next to nothing. I would need more training from the Special New Weapons Division of the Corrupt Instigation Agency (CIA).

To be sure, their ultimate aim (no pun intended) is to weaken our immunity and control our minds. The Establishment and Illuminati know that human beings have an electromagnetic sphere, just like planet Earth. Since humans are born on the planet, we are wired to Earth, and so if they can control the planet's EMF's, it is logical that once the technology is further perfected, they can control us like string puppets, just the only differences are you won't be able to see the strings, and it will much more evil than the plot of a Punch and Judy play.

Now let's discuss the natural side of the planet being full of electromagnetic (EM))zones ranging from very positive to very negative. That is, let me clear in one point of potential confusions: the positive EM zones that are good for health and enhance one's natural EM human field are actually full of negative ions. In reverse, EM zones full of positive ions are mal-aligned to the human EM field because they create 'disturbances' and weaken the immunity of most that live under or in them.

So let me talk a bit about my theory called Electro-Magnetically

Catalyzed Weather (EMCW). This is using the HAARP-based technology and probably even stronger armaments and it is directly and indirectly causing a whole different world of weather. That is, EMCW causes different types of weather storms: the normal ice storm, blizzard, snowstorm, ocean storm, firestorm, dust devil, windstorm, squall, gale, thunderstorm, tropical cyclone, hailstorm, tornado, etc.) and meteorological patterns (unending drought, etc.) are metamorphosized as a result of an electro-magnetic or plasma discharge(s) into the atmosphere. Now, obviously, there are naturally-occurring EMCW events too in which solar / cosmic discharges or ejections (or 'injections') of plasma push through open fissures in the ionosphere and soon after they enter the lower levels of the earth's atmosphere they form a EMCW event.

Now, these kinds of storms are far less predictable differing from the typical storms that are formed by other meteorological means / theories (such as pressure pattern changes, latent heat exchanges, etc.). The main difference between typical weather and EMCW events are as follows:

- QUANTITY/AMOUNT: in an EMCW event, there is a far higher quantity of snow / rain, or enormous hail size or very intense wind forces for a very short time, all setting new historic records;
- FORCE/POWER: an EMCW occasion is more powerful and destructive than typical weather occurrences; in other words, the higher intensity is very notable;
- SPEED/TIMING: an EMCW episode is more sudden and without warning; it is more fast-moving.

Also, there are mystery booms and "weird" noses that many people are hearing all over the world. Some of these are made from tests originating from this electromagnetic weaponry. I'm going to call them sky-quakes, because it literally ripples the atmosphere, and what we are hearing is the sudden acoustical attenuation of shifting electromagnetics in the sky which is also bouncing off the surface. This is not technically a sound-wave, but instead is a vibration-shift of our dimension. This causes all kinds of modifications in our field of space, including temporary wormholes that people can slip into (and literally disappear, most likely forever, unless the 'entrance door' re-emerges in the same exact location and the person sees or more likely senses the change and re-enters). Yeah, it sounds like science fiction, but this is anything but that. The bigger picture of these foreign sounds is that there is a 'war' between the natural dimension coming in and the Establishment trying to stop it with their weaponry. They do not want this new dimension coming in because it is going to evolve the planet for the better.

For example, new technologies, new medicine, and new advancements in many areas will come into the "ether" – into our realm of acknowledgment when this new dimension arrives. So part of the electromagnetic machinery is to try to stop the arrival of this new dimension to keep us enslaved. It's going to be a war of totally new proportions compared to wars in the past. The elite do not value human life. They want to get rid of our consciousness awakening and make us into robots. This is why the field of trans-humanism is coming to light now so much now, and why many in the Mainstream Media are touting it as very cool and how we ought to accept it. This direction is evil: it is not for the advancement of humans. Instead, it is just the opposite. The special groups of the elite are eugenicists. And they are going to get increasingly desperate. As they see more human be-ings awakening, they are going to try to close-out the windows allowing this progress of humanity to occur.

So we are being radiated upon, and the cruel scheme of destroying our immune systems with toxins including radiation just symbolically went into the stratosphere with 2011's Fukushima catastrophe. Another incredibly sick program of eugenics is governments not only not admitting to their incredibly criminal tactics of allowing populations to suffer (aside: read up on the Georgia Guidestones), but also their immoral continuation of such acts in light of verification and substantiation.

There IS mounting evidence that increasing amounts of radiation from Fukushima continues to come into the United States, Europe and other regions / countries. I can state emphatically that as an atmospheric scientist, I am monitoring the amount of radiation in dispersion flow. Since one of my specialties is in electromagnetics, the radiation amounts are becoming intense enough to actually make notable shifts in regional climate patterns. Permit me to explain: moisture coalescence is altered by a shift in atmospheric electromagnetics, and radiative streams is just another way that can interfere with and metamorphosize that equation. The radiation essentially can minimize the grouping of water droplets at the normalized rate without the radiation. Many in mainstream will say this is not true, but I am requesting that we all empower ourselves to learn the truth(s) that continue to show their ugly heads. Obviously, when you get less efficiency of water to bind in the atmosphere, the end result is more drought.

Of course the question comes up, 'why would engineers have put a nuclear power plant on a tectonic fault zone and then mounted the back-up generators in front of the power plant (i.e., closer to the sea, at sea-level)'? Was this done in the grand scheme of design to minimize population longevity by having always a high number of risks, or moreover, was it done to keep populations needy of medical procedures (i.e., have the cancer radiation and chemo business at full throttle in years ahead)? Some will obviously say to me, "You have obviously lost your marbles!" I will always get on any public airwaves and give a logical set of arguments to prove my analysis is sane and backed-up by science. I am certainly glad to see that humanity as a whole is increasingly seeing through the thick veils of fraud, illicit deception and psychological trickery: the few people that allow children, women and men to go through terrible health decay through no fault of their own must be tried in a court of law.

In summary, silent weaponry of the Military Industrial Complex is the 21st-century way of governments dealing with population control by causing immense health challenges. There is a huge challenge in humanity's mental, physical and spiritual condition. There has never been a more important time than now to start your own research and to learn how all governmental manipulation of electromagnetic technology is so cleverly woven together in an intricate web of fabrication and associated directly with weather warfare, lowering our immunity and dumbing us down through brainwashing, cerebral control and blocking our true potential to astral travel and use our mind's beautiful array of abilities yet unseen by most.

Gratitude for starting to be more aware today, using this book (and others) as your seed to better understand the beauty of your brain and ultimately, the most wonderful gift given to each of us human be-ings … the ability of your God-Self to connect to the energetic Oneness of Creation inside each of us.

CHAPTER 13

AVOID THE SCARE TACTICS, EMBRACE THE SUN

Lack Of Sunshine Increases The Risk Of Cancer

We are constantly told to stay out of the sun because its rays are dangerous, especially now that so much of the media blasts-out recycled news about the huge hole in the ozone layer. Doctors and skin experts warn us of the dreadful 'c-word', cancer, that has literally become an epidemic in modern cultures. Everywhere we go shopping, we see aisles of different strengths of sunscreen lotion and other UV "defense" products. SPF5, 15, 30, 50 and probably 100 will come out next, marketed "just for babies", all with the conditioned message for us to lather-up and pour it on in ample quantities.

I am not one to mince words. Over the last few decades and especially in more recent years, there has been an increasingly more dramatic and negative crusade by the Establishment, many departments of allopathic medicine (perhaps led by a classic board-certified neurologically-deranged dermatologist that whips up toxic Botox, and injects other stuff out of syringes), the cosmeceutical industry, and even educators and researchers (centering in on those that are paid to say what their bosses want said) to work together in frightening the bejeezus out of us by telling us to stay out of the sun.

But make no mistake about it, this campaign by authorities to keep us out of the sun is an appalling volume of lies and deception. And it runs so deep that the average advice you get will actually help to kill you. That's right -- when you learn the truth about the toxins involved in the overwhelming majority of allopathic medicine, you will have to wonder how these doctors ever got certified. I thought these medical doctors took the Hippocratic Oath to "never do harm to anyone" and to "prevent disease whenever I can, for prevention is preferable to cure." At least they did follow to that once upon a time. But now, it's all about profit and you, my friend, are just a number. Shoot, most allopathic doctors have truly forgotten the Hippocratic Oath: shame on you Mr. or Ms. Average M.D. No, you are not welcome in my home, and if God forbid I get cancer, I "ain't" coming to get your death-kit "medicine".

The fact is that the sun provides many healing secrets, and the Establishment do not want you knowing them, because if you live longer, you're likely going to cost the Establishment more money to keep you here on this planet.

The fact is the sun elevates your mood, increases your happiness, boosts your energy, decreases illness and wards away germs and pathogens like viruses.

Research the Internet, think for yourself and determine which makes the most logical sense – the allopathic doctor that is dead-set on using toxic pharmaceutical drugs, radiation, chemo and excessive surgery to help 'cure' you of your ailments – or the naturopathic doctor that is using wisdom collected from hundreds if not thousands of years ago and advocates the natural healing abilities of the sun and your body to regulate and heal itself. Make no mistake about it, we are entering a very crucial period where there will be two terribly diverse camps – literally the difference between death and life: those that vilify anyone that doesn't mindlessly accept the path of health in popping toxic pills, eating genetically-modified foods, drinking fluoridated city water, and staying out of the sun – or those that connect the dots, cease the brainwashing, and get on the bandwagon of true health by seeing that the movement toward natural well-being is climaxing higher and higher with every month forward.

Communication From Your Heart Is Key To Your Path

As I emphasize many times in this book, the 'awakening' that many of us must go through now is the necessity to empower yourself and others you love and care about with knowledge about optimizing well-being. After all, the number one necessity to achieve just about anything in life is good health. Ultimately, you are in charge of your health. Your doctor is an advisor, not somebody that can force you to do something. Like I will say later on, your intuition is very important: it is communication from your heart and the omnipotent divine intelligence between your mind and the Universe or Source. So if someone like your doctor is telling you something that does not feel 'right', then you have an obligation to Self to think it through more thoroughly, become more in-tune with your body-mind-heart-soul communication, and make decisions for you, family, and other companions in your life that are in the highest good.

Here is just one nugget that will empower your health and life: if you spend moderate (not excessive of course) amounts of time in the sun, you can actually prevent and even cure skin cancer. You are probably thinking, 'wait a second', that is just the opposite of what my doctor is telling me. That is correct. You may also think, 'well, who are you, Simon Atkins? Why should I believe you?' We all have a choice about what we do. I am laying the seed for you to question what you may not know. I have studied many so-called locked-up secrets of health over the years, and I am asking you to give power to yourself to start a new journey of self-discovery.
The Path to Awakening is the best thing you can do in your life because it is the first part of maximizing Abundance.

Realize that the Establishment and most allopathic doctors think that there is no harm in vaccines, no harm in taking Big Pharma pills, no harm in petroleum-based sunscreen lotions, no harm in putting lithium in your public water supply, no harm in spraying our food crops with carcinogenic pesticides (and the list goes on and on and on). Most of those indirectly or directly controlling your major decisions do NOT have your well-being as their number one priority, period. Of course there are exceptions, and those are the people that make-up your Trust Circle. But we are not here to talk about the exceptions, we are here to talk about the Ultimate Mind Game (UMG) – the last frontier that the Establishment is frantically researching and pouring Trillions (oh yes, much higher than billions; the money that is never printed that remains in a secretive 'vacuum') of dollars to gain control over you by causing you to never question the chip (often referred to as the 'Mark of the Beast' in the Bible) that is scheduled to be put under the skin on your wrist or finger. But 'wait!' you say. You may tell me that you know doctors and people in the government that are good people. And I might agree with you. The real question is: are they Awake? Do they know about the Mind Frontier that the Establishment is getting close to cracking? Do they realize that HAARP, chemtrails, Morgellons Disease, nano-technology inside flu shots, and so much more are all control devices at the ELECTROMAGNETIC level to tap into and further control our energetic realm of functioning??

If you guessed either control or money, you are right, in fact the overwhelming part of allopathic medicine these days is about the corruption of making the organizations fatter in currency, and controlling the patients by making them unhealthier so that the system feeds upon itself. Yes, it is very sick. And perhaps once you start to research this whole mess and go down the big rabbit holes I and many others have entered, you will be just as disgusted as I have become in the absolute sleaze of much of healthcare and the lies it disseminates. Some may think I am angry. Oh no, I went above that: I am doing something about it. I am bringing out the truth to help as many people as I can. I am Awakening, I am

Connecting with One, and let me tell you something, the vibration is incredible. Fortunately, many of you know the same intuitively, but we each must help others become unclouded all for the greater collective good.

Most believe the so-called officials in charge of cleaning-up the Fukushima radiation catastrophe in March of 2011 when they say they are doing their best. It is not the truth, and in actuality, it is far from the truth. We humans are incredibly resourceful and we could have had this incredibly toxic disaster cleaned-up in a matter of a year or less. The world COULD have come together in realizing the incredible magnitude of the negative imbalances of this disaster. We could have put the best minds together, and we could have put any sizeable amount of money to fix this. But the best minds were never listened to. And those in control didn't want the problem fixed. In fact, the "hole" gets much larger than this: research makes it such that the Fukushima disaster looks "suspicious". If I look at this from a scientific point-of-view, after reviewing so many videos when the tsunami was coming into the Japanese coastline, almost none of the buildings were touched by the supposed 9.0 earthquake. A 9.0 Richter Scale earthquake would have flattened so many of the buildings BEFORE the tsunami had reached the coastline, but this was not the case. If you compare the Kobe earthquake, which was still very strong but weaker than the March 11, 2011 megaquake, many buildings were smashed to the ground.

Remember one basic thing: what most are told in the news is less than five percent of what really goes on.

Mind open!

Epilogue

When Other Objects Appear In The Sky

"THE EARTH'S *ATMOSPHERE* DOESN'T BOTHER *ME*, BUT I'M HAVING TROUBLE WITH THE *TIME CHANGE.*"

Epilogue

Perhaps not too long ago, you may have read any number of articles about how more people were occasionally seeing two suns in the sky? Societally, we are trained to quickly dismiss such a story because we convince ourselves quickly that there is only one sun in our sky, and that those that see two must be crazy. Of course, it almost always starts with a simple question: can you really be sure of what you are visually seeing and interpreting in front of you as the reality you think it is?

See, we are 'humming' along a certain electromagnetic frequency. We are dialed-in to a certain station on the universe's radio, and as our sun's light begins to shift or metamorphosize, we too gradually re-align with a new frequency which then literally changes the things we see and the way we see them.

Like a bell curve, there are always going to be the frontrunners who shift their degree of perception first. Because the overwhelming majority have no idea what these people are talking about when they say they see two suns in the sky, they are labeled 'weirdos' or worse. And I would imagine that if they were to march around the White House screaming, "Look, dude, there are two suns in the sky, don't you see 'em?!" then they might very well be befriending a straitjacket after being arrested.

But, see, one's perception of reality is not necessarily the same as another's because most of us are truly not seeing or interpreting what is truly 'out there' in multiple dimensions further than our current 'programmed' brain, which is "trained" in three-dimensions. The so-called rabbit hole of reality goes much deeper than any of us probably can imagine. Everything is shifting all the time. Change is always happening, and therefore change is the norm. Aside, this is why those that welcome change are simply going to be more healthy and more successful and have more ease in attaining true abundance because s/he has mastered one part of going along with the Flow instead of 'fighting' the energetic shift most of the time.

When a large (atmospheric, global, cosmic) magnetic flux is shifting its frequency of reverberation more and more quickly, it will cause or allow something called dimensional 'bending' where "new" dimensions will literally begin to 'pop' into, 'meld' or even 'overtake' our current dimensional 'observational deck'. This cyclical pattern – one that has happened through eons – has already started happening again – and THIS is how evolution at the cosmic level takes place. Evolution takes place at the energetic level: earth transitions in evolutionary stages through shifting dimensional planes. And now, an increasing number of people (especially Star Children and soul groups from far away) are sensitive to these magnificent, yet truly mind-blowing deviations from "normal" (if there is ever an ordinary).

So permit me to repeat myself from an earlier chapter: when the FDA tells you don't go out into the sun, I cannot force you but I urge you to do all you can not to listen. The FDA is steering you the wrong way. The sun is giving off important energy at this time to accelerate our Awakening. Our pineal gland needs these rays, for mental, emotional and spiritually-guided well-being and holistic advancement. Of course, I am advising to be out in the sun in moderation: do not sun-bathe for hours and hours at the beach nor be on top of a mountain without the necessary clothes, head, eye and lip protection otherwise you will get sunstroke, sick or worse. I am talking about temperance when it comes to soaking in the solar energy. The "sun-worship" must be done gradually, but frequently, and can be attained from walking, gardening, bird-watching, or just merely working outdoors.

Some have already reported seeing two (binary) suns (or "day" stars) in the sky. Sometimes, there are other objects in space too – both celestial and of other worlds. This phenomenon could be natural as caused by the pre-stated intermittent dimensional bending. You could be looking right into or right through another dimension. That is, quite literally, another dimension harboring another star (or object) is entering our field of vision. Or this could be a complex technological, panoramic, large hologram, similar to the one used on 9/11/11 over New York City.

The Elite know all about this, and it is time for us to catch-up so We the People have the advantage. Read Sun Tzu's "Art of War" to know how strategy plays a huge role in which side has the ability to determine the desired outcome. Of course, my desire is to dismantle the weaponry of the side that is playing its hand against us. And through this disassembling of negativity, we can choose a new path for humanity that will allow for prosperity not enslavement at the energetic level.

And now I leave you with these important words, that will have more significance in the future when certain events happen … which I will discuss with a lot of detail in *Skyaia®: Blinded or Awake?, Volume 2*, which will be published soon.

Most of you may be interested in why you're feeling the way you are lately: you may have periods of increased weariness, emotional exhaustion, short-term memory issues, hot flashes beyond hormonal imbalances, objects entering from side vision, and many more "oddities" that will make some query if they are going insane. Unless you are truly ill (physically and/or mentally), the source of these physical and cerebral changes are very likely the opening and shifting of the inter-dimensionality of Earth's magnetic field causing an "evolutionary" shift in consciousness. More are becoming sensitive to these changes. *Volume 2 of Skyaia®: Blinded or Awake?* will address these shifts in-depth.

Another set of symptoms directly related to the perturbations of the planetary and our own magnetic fields are distinct changes in how you hold short-term memory – because literally, memory is a function of the magnetics of our own nervous system and that of Earth. Our brains process information through the minute gravitational and non-gravitational fields of its own structure and it is affected directly by fluctuations in the earth's magnetic field. And so you can expect an increase in short term memory anomalies. You may find yourself speaking a sentence and suddenly the words do not come to you or you mix up the words from their normal syntax. While in some extreme cases this could be the sign of a brain disorder, it is very likely you have nothing of the sorts, but you will find cerebral changes happening within the general populace at an increasing rate. Escalations in collective short-term memory glitches will lead humanity to a most novel situation. This situation is an opportunity or a curse, depending on how you work with it.

The opportunity is to see through the mental matrix of your own creation. What is meant by this is when your mind is unable to continue its story line in the ways it is used to, you have an opportunity to glimpse the realities behind the curtain (of perception). We are the ones who have created the curtain, and we have done this to keep ourselves separated from things that we do not wish to see or experience directly, or in some cases what others do not wish us to see or experience directly. This is the unseen manipulators of our collective reality—those who hold the economic and political reins of power.

There are forces on our planet that actively resist the impulse for spiritual evolution. They are invested in continuing their lies through the misappropriation of information in order to control us. Their job is getting more difficult because the perturbation of the magnetic field creates gaps in the creation of mental realities projected by the human mind. They – meaning those who wish to control and manipulate you – have vast resources at their command, and they are employing every one of them. But they cannot quickly control the magnetic field of the earth! For sure they are trying to – and that is why HAARP and other higher-intensity programs exist.

The impulse that is affecting the magnetic field of the earth comes from far beyond their locus of influence. It might be an expectation, based upon the understanding one day of hyper-dimensional physics, that the perturbations of our magnetic field are going to increase over the next several years. Those of us who are sensitive energetically are the ones feeling this most intensely at the present moment, but I suspect that in the next two to three years most people will be affected by this in a way they are consciously aware of, even if they do not know why.

There are a couple of suggestions for dealing with the situation. The first suggestion is the easiest. It involves understanding your connection to the core of the earth itself. As an energetic being, in addition to your flesh and blood, we each can form a conscious energetic relationship with the core of the earth. This understanding, or orientation, is that you are immersed in and surrounded by earth's magnetic field. By going into mental resonance with the core of the earth (the generator of earth's magnetic field), you become energetically stabilized. The earth, as a conscious entity, can reveal

Herself to you in ways that are difficult to describe because our culture does not have a language for this. And we have been manipulated and controlled to insure that we do not have an awareness of this, for it could be one of our greatest strengths. By entering into resonance with the core of the earth you become more conscious of the earth as a living conscious be-ing (aka The Gaia Theory). Through this link, you receive a type of energetic-solidity – even in the midst of earth's increasing chaos. The odd thing about it, however, is that when you bring yourself to your senses, so to speak, you are less controllable, less coerced by those forces that control the thought stream of humanity through mis-information, manipulation and mind-control. In other words, forming a direct conscious relationship with the earth's core bypasses many of the effects of what might be known as life-negative technologies.

If you wish to do something in addition to entering into mental resonance with the core of the earth, a first suggestion is using your pranic tube, a subtle energetic channel that runs from above your head, through the center of your body, and into the earth. This tube, this channel, can be extended deep into the earth, down into the very core itself, and also above the head deep into space. In this method you are not dealing with extending the channel beyond the top of the head. Instead, you only extend the channel into the core of the earth. But the essential thing is not so much the sending of this channel into the earth. The essential thing is to understand that you are in resonance with the core of the earth simply by knowing it. This will impart a sense of stability even in the midst of increasing chaos. It will awaken your senses. It will bring you into a greater conscious relationship to earth. Yet with some caution, it will also de-hypnotize you – make you less controllable. And you will see through the lies around you more clearly! This can be very startling at first; you will likely first have feelings of anger, and you will question why you have been lied to for your entire life.

The second suggestion involves developing a conscious relationship to the core of the galaxy. Essentially, understand that you can be in resonance with the core of the Milky Way Galaxy, which is part of a black hole, and that in similar ways to being in resonance with the core of the earth, you can become stabilized in relationship to the galaxy. If you are capable of this, simply hearing this described to you will activate the knowingness of how to do it.

These suggestions may seem like a complex affair. But, most importantly, they require the understanding that a part of you is not limited by the time and space coordinates of your physical body. It requires an understanding that consciousness can extend instantaneously, anywhere in time and space, and by extending your consciousness to the galactic core, you are stabilized in relationship to the galaxy. The ideal is to be in relationship to earth's core and the core of the galaxy simultaneously. Then you will be able to ride the waves of energy from deep space with a greater degree of mastery.

This will make you less governable and harder to hypnotize, and then you may have the very odd experience of "waking-up" while many around you are still unfortunately "asleep".

SPECIAL NOTE

Skyaia: Blinded or Awake? Volume 2

♦ To Be Published Soon ♦

In *Volume 2 – Skyaia®: Blinded or Awake?*, the first section will delve into a part of your life that is so important – and that is to "Intent Your Freedom" (i.e., you literally have to command your freedom before you can manifest abundance or even know what you truly desire in the Universe, including realizing your purpose). This conversation will include advanced revelations in *how* to enhance your life in order to receive so much more abundance in health, love and wealth. The second part will be all about "Moving Into A New Light" where each of us can better understand our human origins, the space-time conundrum of why we are "trapped" – continually 'fed' into war and fear, and how we can reach the new goal of facing each day protecting our God-given rights to freedom, love and peace.

A MULTI-LAYERED CANCER CURE

I will provide a wealth of information on the vibration of our cells and offer a 'multi-plane' solution for cancer. I am not accepting the lies, poisoning, corruption and deception of Big Pharma anymore. As a team effort, we have to connect the dots to better our own health, and in saying so, I feel very strongly in sharing with the world the solution, therapy, and healing for cancer. The chains holding us hostage to sickness must be broken and our health freedom must be individually and societally grasped before it slips away.

In addition, I will discuss very rational and healthy process of communicating with departed loved ones. The second section will then start by concentrating on achieving energetic or life-force health, which will be followed by talking about something that so many of us may want to discuss more – extraterrestrial life – and the huge exposé on what is happening on our planet. I push you, the reader and my humanitarian comrade, much further, in asking you to officially take off the blindfold that has been put on just about every one of us since a child. Then one of my dear friends will share something so radical about what actually happened on that fateful day we all refer to as 9/11.

The last two chapters of Volume 2 will deliberate on our future by telling about "our greatest challenge ever" coming down the road. To meet this test of humanity, I describe how we have to interlink new energetic forces as both technology negativities and our cerebral awareness increase. I will also provide communal consulting in order to allow more networking in discovery and healing of this transformative process.

I am truly humbled by the incredible outreach of all connecting to the words and thoughts that bridge us all to these commonalities described within these pages.

What you do with this awareness is, of course, your choice and your response-ability.

So in joining energetically dear brothers and sisters all over the world, as you breathe deeply and beckon peace from above, I say unto thee, Namaste and Amen for now.

Connect with @DrSimonAtkins on Twitter and give me a shout out for a follow back!

Visit www.Skyaia.com to see the list of chapters in Volume 2 and join the Skyaia® Community in the blog section to find out more about how you can help yourself, your family, others you care about, and your planet in creating more abundance, peace and love.

Recommended Books / Papers, A Short List

Market Timeless Secrets Of Health & Rejuvenation: Breakthrough Medicine For the 21st Century, by Andreas Moritz.

The Five Bodies, by J.J. Hurtak, Ph.D. with Desiree Hurtak, MS.Sc. (The Academy for Future Science, 1994).

The Book of Knowledge: The Keys of Enoch, by J.J. Hurtak (The Academy for Future Science, 1977).

Cancer Is Curable Now and Healing Cancer With Common Sense, by Marcus & Sabrina Freudenmann

The Gerson Therapy: The Proven Nutritional Program For Cancer and Other Illnesses, by Charlotte Gerson and Morton Walker

The Healing Energies Of Earth, by Liz Simpson.

The Gods' Machines, by Wun Chok Bong.

365 Tao, by Deng Ming-Dao.

As A Man Thinketh: Discover How Your Thoughts Create Your Reality, by James Allen.

Playing The Field: Geomagnetic Storms and the Stock Market, by Anna Krivelyova (Boston College) and Cesare Robotti (Federal Reserve Bank of Atlanta)

Exultation is the going
of an inland soul to sea,
Past the houses – past the headlands –
Into deep Eternity …

◆

Emily Dickinson

www.ingramcontent.com/pod-product-compliance
Lightning Source LLC
Chambersburg PA
CBHW052103230426
43671CB00011B/1918